RAMBLING ACROSS AMERICA

The Tale of One Country Boy's Unstoppable Dream

TOMMY RAY

Copyright Information

Rambling Across America: The Tale of One Country Boy's Unstoppable Dream.

Copyright © 2017 by Tommy Ray.

No part of the book may be used or reproduced in any manner whatsoever without the written permission of the author, except in the case of brief quotations embodied in critical articles and reviews. For information, contact the author at tommy@tommyraybooks.com

Book Cover Design: Judith San Nicolas
http://www.judithsdesign.com/#home

Developmental Editor: Patricia Smith
https://www.linkedin.com/in/patricia-b-smith-035a8813

Editor: Nadia Bruce-Rawlings
https://www.amazon.com/Nadia-Bruce-Rawlings/e/B00RKSRW6U

Proofreader: Daniel Johnson
https://reedsy.com/daniel-johnson

Formatting: Joel Pitney
joel@launchmybook.com

ISBNs
Print: 9789082820713
eBook: 9789082820706

Printed in the United States of America

Interior design by booknook.biz

GRATITUDE PAGE

I wish to express gratitude and thankfulness concerning the adventure of the "Confessions of a Dreamer Tour."

- The inaugural night in Natchez, Mississippi.
- Complimentary nights of camping underneath the stars.
- My Aunt Jo and Uncle Roy for regularly opening their home.
- The readers who extended support along with friendship daily, thank you!
- To those along the road who provided a place to lodge, a hot shower, as well as fabulous meals. Your friendships filled my heart with joy and happiness.
- Importantly, God, who guarded the tour with safeness, yielded necessities, and allowed me to accomplish the journey.

DISCLAIMER

Rambling Across America: The Tale of One Country Boy's Unstoppable Dream chronicled events traveling on the "Confessions of a Dreamer Tour." It reflected opinions relating to those experiences. Some names coupled with identifying details of individuals mentioned have been altered to protect their privacy.

"Congratulations! Today is your day. You're off to Great Places! You're off and away!"
—Dr. Seuss

CHAPTER 1

CONFESSIONS OF A DREAMER

I have often thought of myself as odd, an outsider, or sometimes even a misfit. My perspective of the world conveyed differently than most. I desired to live a life among a creative plane instead of a competitive one. I believed there was plenty for everyone, a Universe of abundance. I longed for financial freedom along with location independence comparable to the masses, yet, I wished to achieve this differently than most. I desired to utilize the imagination as well as creativity to inspire and deliver value to the world. I craved adventure. I yearned for journeys. God created an amazing world. I believed it was my intention to taste, touch, see, and hear everything I could. I visualized myself on pilgrimages carrying a backpack or in an RV traveling. Though I pondered a home base; a site to be used to rest or to write blogs and books about the adventures as I planned new ones. Mostly, I was in motion. I wished to act in a certain way.

As a small child, mostly alone, I utilized my imagination to enhance my daily adventures. When I became an adult, I disagreed it must stop. I trusted there was always a child inside of us requiring play as well as fun. Through maintaining a child's curiosity, the world maintained a magical realm.

Though I may have followed the norm a majority of my adult life, the inner voice always whispered, "continue your curiosity." The year of 2012 was the initial onset of truly listening. I decided to resign a position most stated was a dream job. I was employed as a physician assistant. My employer was the team physician for two Major League Baseball Teams. With the resignation, I was called a fool by numerous individuals, including family. Nonetheless, I yearned to journey on a pilgrimage. Through unwavering faith, prayer, along with research, I departed from the norm. I walked the Camino de Santiago, "A Country Boy on the Camino." Unfortunately, in November of the same year, I returned to the path everyone stated was the correct path. I attempted to adjust myself back "into the mold," so to speak. Nevertheless, the entire time I was at work at a "regular" job, my dreams along with the road were always calling to me. The voice denied being held silent.

Again, in late 2015, I returned to my inner self for guidance. The result was the "Confessions of a Dreamer Tour" described in the following pages.

The most popular question I was asked was "Why abandon security for uncertainty?" After pondering the question, my response was simple: "Why not, life was short; get busy living or get busy dying," inspired by the movie *Shawshank Redemption*.

CHAPTER 2

SEED OF CHANGE

The initial seed of change developed in May of 2014. I began the transformation after listening to Rhonda Byrne's *The Secret*. I read books by Paulo Coelho, (*The Alchemist* & *Warrior of the Light*), Wallace D. Wattles (*The Science of Getting Rich*), among others. I watched motivational channels by Jim Rohn, Les Brown, and Evan Carmichael on YouTube. I subscribed to a daily email newsletter, *Tiny Buddha*.

Due to the daily routine of listening to inspirational videos on YouTube as well as the readings, I was confident I had planted seeds into my subconscious mind to live the life I'd imagined. The first affirmative acknowledgement transpired over a year later. I remembered a dream, possibly from August 2015. The daily practice formulated the dream I had experienced. I awoke with the memory of traveling across the United States of America, performing music on the streets as the public gathered around and playing inside intimate venues. With opened eyes peering up at the darkened ceiling along with a beating heart, I conjured up the vivid colors of the dream and the excitement of the scenario. Though the alarm clock displayed 2:30 am, I grasped my bedside journal, writing as much as I could. I recalled images of driving through majestic mountains, observing the Pacific Ocean, performing on street corners or live venues sharing the music I composed.

After completing the writing session, I was curious how others dreamed. Most dreams for me were vivid in color, intense, heart-pounding, with the sensation of legitimacy. Usually I awakened, rarely recalling a single detail. Other times, I could evoke details to record them into a journal. How do you dream?

I continued to ponder the lingering dream daily for the next few weeks. I asked, "Was it possible?" Per Les Brown, "It's possible." Based on a routine study of material about the laws of attraction, dreaming big, the shortness of life, etc., I began to affirm. With thought and prayer, I deliberately decided how to prosper. I chose to emulate a favorite quote by Thoreau: "Go confidently in the direction of your dreams. Live the life you've imagined."

Thoreau's quote, along with words of wisdom from people I respected such as Jim Rohn, Michael Jordan, Steve Jobs, Tony Robbins, Warren Buffet, Bill Gates, Les

Brown, and Jim Carrey, led to me transforming my life. Instead of simply breezing through on hope as I had always done, Warren Buffet advised people to "do what you want to do as if independently wealthy." Me, what I yearned to do, what I constantly craved to undertake, was to travel and write. Go abroad to places like China, Japan, Ireland, Scotland, among others. I desired to be inspired by God's creations of landscapes and architecture. I hungered to compose songs and author books about the travel adventures. To create inspiration, purpose, and value for others all around the world. I longed to help people, perhaps simply by paying for someone's groceries or by ensuring my Mom was provided for. My intention was for the income from the songs along with the books to support the travels and philanthropy. I dreamed to create value and inspire the world.

None of this came out of the blue. I had a history of manifesting my dreams. For everything important in my life, I can recall the point when I prayed for the experience to happen. As a child, I prayed to be in a TV commercial. In 1999, I was flown out to Beverly Hills, California to be a principal actor in a Saturn car commercial. I remember visualizing living in Colorado, as well as overseas. Both happened. When I was a freshman at Guilford College. I was in Mary Broo's office, the Head Athletic Trainer for the athletics department. I looked upon her memory board from her participation as a Certified Athletic Trainer for the Olympics. I declared to myself to somehow be part of the Olympics. In 2002, I was part of the Salt Lake City Winter Olympics as a certified athletic trainer on the medical staff.

I share these experiences to prove to you it was possible to manifest dreams in your own life. How often do you take a moment from your day and imagine a different life, daydream about what you truly want, or wish things could be different? What are you doing to make the things you dream about come true in your life?

CHAPTER 3

THE INTERNET

The first objective was to research options of a journey of such magnitude. First, I conducted internet searches consisting of top live music city locations, ones that favored street busking cities and had dominant songwriter cities. I accumulated the information from websites generated by Google and crafted a list of cities I aspired to visit. The original list comprised of over 100 cities throughout the entire United States. Then, I marked each city on a map. Looking at the marked locations, I generated a chosen route to link the cities. Please take into consideration the present moment of the preliminary researching phase. The final tour had no commitments or time frames for completion, allowing for the freedom of no deadlines once the tour began. To make the dream into reality, I would have to resign from my current job, with only the tour and the unknown ahead. Thus, I was designing an adventure covering the entire United States with no deadline. At such a moment, I had a rough idea of the drivable route. The fantasy tour began in Mississippi, ventured west to California, north to Washington state, then east, moving towards the most north-eastern regions, then south towards Florida, visiting the Keys, completing the loop back to Mississippi. It was greatly overwhelming to visualize the overall route.

Suddenly, I had a course, a blueprint. I was filled with enthusiasm. A country boy had shaped a music tour, on paper, which I had only dreamed about previously.

Next, I formulated a pros and cons list, or "Should I resign the physician assistant position or remain." The inner argument of the ego began. The negatives on the list consisted of the financials and the unknown future. The pros were to follow big dreams, as well as the "life was short" beliefs I had attained from the daily inspirational videos. I questioned how I was going to handle the debt (primarily school loans and current credit cards), meet current bills (rent, food, fuel, fun), and manage the journey. With each thought of "I cannot," I recalled a passage from Rhonda Byrne: "It's not our responsibility to worry about the how; simply ask, believe, receive." Her tone had consistently been expressed by Les Brown, Tony Robbins, Will Smith, and the Bible. The underlying message I perceived was unwavering faith and trust.

THE INTERNET

Over the next several weeks leading into the holiday season of 2015, I prayed and persisted in the daily teachings of the makeshift guru circle I had assembled from YouTube, books, and journaling my thoughts and emotions. I often meditated and listened to my heart along with my gut instincts.

Blessfully, I had an entire week off for Thanksgiving. I embraced the positivity. It was available for decision making. I escaped to a friend's deer camp about an hour and a half from my home. There was no phone service or internet, and the camp consisted of 180 acres of woods and wildlife. My adventures consisted of waking up early for a deer hunt, afternoon walks, an evening hunt, grilling out, 4-wheeling, with continued reading and writing. The hunting aspect allowed me to be 25-feet up in a tree in silence, just listening to the wind. Honestly, I saw deer and never pulled my bow back. It was the time valued in peace and solitude I cherished. The afternoon walks provided focus to remain present. I paid attention only to the sounds, smells, and sights of nature instead of the multiple what-ifs of the decision. For guidance, I took notice of instincts, what I regarded as the voice of God. I possessed faith and believed in the power of prayer.

Five days elapsed with those activities. A decision was reached. The decision was not announced on ESPN as if I were Lebron James; all the same, *I* knew. It was an important aspect. I was at peace and trusted in God.

Once I made the decision, I simply relaxed and declared everything was going to be okay. I would not allow fear to clutch at me. Most importantly, I believed in myself. By taking a leap of faith and confidently believing in the power of my dreams for a different life. I truly sensed I was defining myself. I moved from a life of routine to living a meaningful life. I understood when I started it was going to be difficult, filled with set-backs, failures, and doubt. But I never let it deter me from my path. No matter how bad things got out on the road, I knew I was going to be okay. I had passion, clarity, faith, and of course, desire. It was all the fuel I needed.

The next significant hurdle I had was to discipline myself not to care what others thought. Their negativity may derail ambitions or the path abruptly. It was human nature to desire to be accepted, to be part of the social norm. I decided, rather, to pursue dreams and remain true to my inner self than to adhere to the status quo and other's expectations. A crucial objective was to continue advancing forward and not give up. I recognized I had the faith required to manifest those dreams to reality. I had experienced dreams coming true previously. I knew I had the power to make it all transpire. It was possible. Everyone on YouTube and the authors I followed had created their own desires. Besides, I had asked for certain dreams and desires in my life already, and they appeared: being an actor on a TV commercial, having a role on the medical staff of two professional sports teams

THE INTERNET

and the Olympics, owning the Jeep I love, living in all the places I had lived.

The initial practical step was to truly commit to the decision. I recalled Will Smith stating, "There was no plan B, only plan A." I had a vision which included lofty expectations. I declared that if I desired something, I simply had to persist to obtain it. So, I elected to resign the physician assistant teaching position to pursue traveling, writing books, and composing music full-time. I was aware it might have sounded drastic and erratic. However, I didn't decide overnight! The original intention was to resign after the spring semester, in May of 2016. In those months I could save money as well as decide the tour's details. At least, that was my reasoning leading into December 2015.

Yet, as the month progressed, I decided I wanted to pursue the dream earlier. The constant input, day after day, from motivational videos as well as journaling reflections and ambitions, contributed to a profound idea. I decided to resign earlier. Rather than remaining till May, I mulled over resigning in advance of the spring semester commencing in January. My hesitancy was to not burn professional bridges with a last moment resignation, the five months worth of savings I would miss, along with losing the extra time to blueprint the tour. Nonetheless, the morning of January 5th, 2016, after I tuned into Jim Rohn, "How to live a happy life and take risks, life is short," I elected to resign. At the closure of the workday,

I stepped down and requested to leave the next day. I was granted permission. I had given "personal reasons" and they agreed. I motored home afterward, feeling like a load of cinderblocks had been lifted from my shoulders.

Dinner was tantalizing. I had made the decision. I simply relaxed and told myself everything was going to be okay. I would not allow fear to hold me back. Most importantly, I believed in myself. I knew I would have to work on my skills daily, including writing and practicing guitar. The major goal was to keep moving forward and not give up. I knew I had the faith required to bring my dreams to life. I knew dreams could come true. I had the power to make all of it happen. It was possible.

Henry Ford once said, "The man who said he can and the man who said he cannot are both right." I concluded that I had the strength to develop into the man I envisioned. I understood immediately upon starting it would be difficult, teeming with set-backs, failures, and self-doubt. At no time would it deter me from the path I had selected. No matter how grim the conditions on the route. I trusted I would be fine.

The reality of it all hit the next day while planning the adventure.

CHAPTER 4

DEVISING A TOUR

The next several days were filled with carrying out activities in the apartment, like cleaning. I cleaned the apartment beginning at the top. Then, I cleared away my to-do list items which required completion. Once done, I concentrated on the impending tour.

Considering it would be the first music tour ever attempted by this country boy, I constructed a rough draft checklist of items required. The draft consisted of financials, locations to stopover, venues or streets to perform, and connections I had in the chosen cities.

I began with the financials. I needed an overview of the situation. A single one-week check from my ex-employer arrived in eight days. That alone couldn't settle the January bills. I had sufficient free cash for food in our fast-food era for two weeks. I performed an overview of all available funds. I possessed two credit cards. One credit card contained a zero balance with a $10,000 limit, and an additional credit card with $15,000 available but a current balance of $12,000. I pondered withdrawing the job's retirement fund, with a harsh penalty. It would be about $10,000 in cash afterwards. Finally, the personal retirement fund of $20,000, though IRS tax penalties existed.

Looking over the current monthly bills of school loans, credit card debt, and basic living requirements, I had no alternative: withdraw the work's retirement fund. The release of funds transfer was executed in two weeks. My desired departure date was early March to ensure the weather would be warmer. This allowed for vacating the apartment to reduce the monthly bills during the tour without penalty of breaking a lease.

I had a baseline of the financials available for living. I had adequate funds to meet the debt for January and February. However, I had merely given thought to the funds required prior to the tour, not by any means considering the tour itself or my future.

I scrutinized the monthly bills to detect if anything at all may be discontinued to reduce the required money disappearing. I decided it was most fitting to procure forbearance of the school loans from the three degrees I had achieved. Overall, I'd incurred $220,000 in student loan debt, which equaled a monthly payment of $1500. Nearly all could be deferred six months to a year. After the deferment process, I reduced the monthly payment from $1500 to $400, for the next six months. The negative was, of course, new interest increased the overall amount borrowed.

Next was to generate a monetary estimate for the tour. The original tour was planned for the entire United States of America with no time frame. Consequently, I was notified I had been nominated for two music awards by the Mississippi Music Foundation. The nominations comprised the best artists of Mississippi as well as the best songwriters. The awards show was May 6th, 2016 in Southaven, Mississippi. So, the tour would be launched in March, but terminate prior to the awards show on May 6th. Knowing the time frame gave me the ability to be specific on my overhead.

I titled the tour, "Confessions of a Dreamer." My financial obligations consisted of food, fuel, lodging, and preparation. I guessed the amount required. In 2012, I had trekked the Camino de Santiago. It was a pilgrimage following the same steps of St. James, a disciple of Jesus. The journey began in St. Jean de Port, France and ended in Muxia, Spain. I walked over 600 miles in his footsteps in 40 days. I spent less than $2,000. My adventure, "A Country Boy On The Camino," was documented on Amazon by means of an E-book. Knowing a previous adventure had been $2000, I believed I could do the tour on roughly the same amount. The intent was to acquire money pursuing the dream through street busking and profits from the EP "Crossroads." The proceeds would provide food and shelter.

Two components were now checked: the route and the financials. Neither were predetermined precisely; nevertheless, a crude estimation was better than nothing.

The next question: by what method to arrange a tour? Originally, I thought I would literally travel to each city, search out a street, and commence jamming. The crowd would donate money for food as well as lodging. Then with a flash, I thought perhaps I may be capable of a prepared tour. The venues would schedule an appearance, paying this country boy to perform. Google became my friend. I randomly explored terms, such as how to tour, songwriter venues located among the cities to visit, locales to street perform, and best venues for live music. Of course, millions of websites appeared. I decided upon websites citing lists related to primary live songwriting venues or locales along with essential tour design. I conducted the inquiry for each location. I generated an excel sheet: it catalogued the venues' names, locations, contact persons, instructions, contact information. I preferred the venues I was capable of emailing. I dispatched over 100 emails to the venues who sought the style of music I performed. Each email stated a brief "Confessions of a Dreamer" mission statement. Four weeks lapsed; not a single venue replied. I was very disheartened. Still, I realized, there was always the street and open mics.

I progressed daily, reviewing motivational material of favorite authors. I established a daily ritual of studying Paulo Coelho's *The Alchemist* and *Warrior of the Light*, a once

DEVISING A TOUR

daily email from Tiny Buddha, along with subscriptions of 15 plus motivation channels on YouTube. Those channels encompassed lectures furnished by previous listed individuals as well as "Your World Within," "HESMotivation," and "Evan Carmichael," to identify a few. Those instruments of knowledge enhanced the positive and optimistic attitude: "It is possible." I improved my wisdom with an optimistic perspective. I modified my ideology. Material on the laws of attraction enhanced the aspiration to succeed with daily journaling, formation of vision boards, and prayer. I practiced gratitude, thankfulness, and appreciation of what I currently had. I possessed unwavering faith that I could transform my life, and furthermore, experience location independence and financial freedom. Dreams were converting into reality. I placed confidence in Jim Rohn: "Time is more valuable than money. You can get more money, but you can't get more time." Life was brief, tune into the heart and place trust in your instincts. Relish life. Impose the mind to triumph.

Of course, a multitude of family and friends stated it was impossible. I ignored them and advanced on the dream. I was carrying out what 99% of the population were not achieving: to savor a life. I trusted and commanded the best of myself to live a life I desired. I visualized each dream, living as if they were already legitimate. I simply believed.

During February, I spent time packing the apartment. I had arranged to vacate the apartment the first week of

March. With each packed box, I had to decide between items required for the tour and items to be packed into storage. I also had to keep in mind possessions reserved for long-term storage versus temporary storage. Those short-term items would be necessary when I returned in May. I contemplated what supplies would be needed for the tour itself. Those provisions would have to fit into the truck: my new home.

I thought of the tour as an extended camping trip. I thought of provisions a person would require. I contemplated necessities for cooking and sleeping, along with the gadgets required to perform on the streets. I developed a rough-draft checklist. I confirmed many things which I already had. I composed a to-buy list. Luckily, I had nearby a Bass Pro Shop, a Dick's Sporting Goods, and everyone's favorite, Wal-Mart. On the list was a cooking stove, sleeping bag, battery powered amp, amongst others.

I would have to vacate the apartment soon. To improve the truck, I purchased a waterproof lockable bed cover. It would protect belongings from theft as well as from being destroyed by weather.

After vacating the apartment, I became a guest of Aunt Jo and Uncle Roy. Aunt Jo was the younger sister to Tommy G. Ray, my deceased father. They resided in Pearl, Mississippi. Their home was approximately twenty minutes from the apartment. The visit with them lasted about a week until the tour commenced.

DEVISING A TOUR

My father never witnessed me strum a guitar or vocalize a note. Unfortunately, he passed away in 2002 before I picked up the guitar or even dreamed about performing.

The week visiting the relatives went by quickly. Each day was consumed with loading and unloading the truck. The space was filled meticulously. Final supplies were purchased as I thought of them. The positive was that Aunt Jo prepared exceptional food each night. The favorites in her kitchen were green beans, fried okra, squash with onions, and cornbread baked in an iron skillet. Each night I appreciated the home-cooked meal as well as the queen-sized bed in their guest room. On the tour, the intent was to bed down in the backseat a considerable amount. The meals would be primarily what could be cooked on the butane stove I had purchased. The idea was to remain under $2,000.

2009 Toyota Pre-Runner, "The Silver Horse I Ride."

CHAPTER 5

MARCH 15, 2016

The journey launched in less than 24-hours. I had transformed the 2009 Toyota Pre-Runner into a new home. In the words of Bon Jovi, it was "the silver horse I ride."

The last day was spent executing the final preparations for the tour, preparing the truck itself and the supplies. I converted the back seat of the truck into a bunk. I considered a tent. Instead, I thought sleeping in the truck in strange places versus the outdoors in a tent was safer. I arranged red cotton sheets over the seat cushions for protection, along with increased padding. I stowed two pillows as well as a sleeping bag. The sleeping bag would be used as the blanket. I elected to haul a bicycle. I purchased a lockable bicycle support system from Yakima. I selected the Ridgeback. It locked into the hitch and was crafted from steel. I strapped the mountain bike to the truck. The bike would provide uncomplicated transportation in unfamiliar cities. It would also be used when I chose to slow down the pace to appreciate the allure of nature God had provided along the route.

The final evening was spent with family prior to embarking on the adventure. Aunt Jo provided a marvelous farewell home-cooked meal. The supper consisted of huge portions of fresh canned green beans, stewed squash and onions, black-eyed peas, and of course, cornbread baked in an iron skillet, all washed down with Southern sweet ice-tea.

As I relaxed afterward, appreciating family, I realized something. The dream from six months prior was now reality. I had dreamed of driving across America, performing original songs in venues or on the streets busking, using the experiences to continue the "Country Boy" travel series. The first E-book was "A Country Boy on the Camino," about the pilgrimage on the Camino de Santiago in 2012. I was about to commence another adventure: "The Confessions of a Dreamer Tour."

I retired to the guest room as the moonlight shone through the curtains. I slipped into the spongy queen-size bed. I pulled the comforter to my chin as I reflected. My resolution to resign my position to pursue dreams had brought me fear and doubt. I aspired to devote time on this earth, to "go confidently in the direction of your dreams," as stated by Thoreau. The moment of departure was imminent. I could not fathom what the future held.

MARCH 15, 2016

I could easily reconsider the field of medicine, yet, I concluded, I preferred to be homeless and chasing dreams than settling with regret. Life was fleeting! I trusted God for an exquisite existence. I clenched my blue eyes, reciting a prayer. *"I persist to sustain unwavering faith. To maintain simple mottos taught by others like, 'what would you do if you knew you could not fail and what would you do if you were independently wealthy.'"* I delighted in orthopedic surgery. I had weathered many struggles to become a physician assistant. Nevertheless, I would rather travel the world, author books, compose music, and bring value and inspiration to the world. I drifted into slumber. Tomorrow was a new day!

The Natchez-Vidalia Bridge over the Mississippi River

CHAPTER 6

MARCH 16, 2016

I awoke on Wednesday morning. I opened my blue eyes to the sunshine filling the room. The original intention had been to leave first thing in the morning. However, I perceived something surprising about myself. Rather than excitement, I felt sluggish. I chose to linger in bed. The blankets shrouded me. The covering ministered protection along with safety. I resembled a small child, curled in a ball, afraid of the monster in the closet.

The aroma of sausage, bacon and scrambled eggs concocted by Aunt Jo was the catalyst I needed. The distinctive smell wafted through the house. The blanket thrown off, lounge wear thrown on, sandals slipped into, and the bedroom door opened as I shuffled into her kitchen. I indulged in a heavenly breakfast, sharing conversation with her and Uncle Roy. Deep down I knew they did not want this country boy to go. Nevertheless, they were positively supportive. They expressed blessings through prayer.

The first destination was less than two hours south. I was driving on the Natchez Trace to Natchez, Mississippi. I loaded last minute luggage into the "steel horse I ride." I embraced Aunt Jo and Uncle Roy. Then I started the truck and backed out of the concrete driveway. I waved goodbye; the "Confessions of a Dreamer Tour" was launched.

I advanced to the on-ramp of the Natchez Trace. It was a twenty-minute drive from Pearl, Mississippi. I loaded the CD *Hero* by Rhonda Byrne and began the adventure.

The Natchez Trace Parkway overall was a 444-mile recreational road and scenic drive through three states. It was two-lanes of asphalt derived from Mississippi red clay. I was driving the lower section from Jackson, Mississippi to Natchez, Mississippi. The distance was 113 miles.

The ramble to Natchez was delightful. The two-lane roadway was winding with overhanging lichened trees. I passed over streams and creeks like the Mud Island Creek, Bullen Creek, and the Turpin Creek. Because of the late start, I did not stop to explore any trails or trek to observe the Owens Creek Waterfall. I almost paused at a free campsite roughly an hour outside of Jackson. It was at the Grand Gulf Military Monument. It offered a secure area to park a vehicle. There was a shower house along with bathrooms. A fire ring was at each parking area to forge a fire. The camping area provided biking and walking trails along the banks of the Mississippi River. Despite the allure, it provided no cell phone service. So, I forged ahead towards Natchez.

Approximately ten miles outside of Natchez was the Natchez State Park. I debated staying the night there, though, with an $18 camping fee, I decided against it and advanced into the city of Natchez. The time was about 5:30 p.m. The original budget strategy was to remain under $2,000 as I had on the Camino de Santiago journey. To accomplish the achievement meant sleeping in the truck and preparing my own meals most days.

I arrived in Natchez. I toured around in the truck for about a half-hour before discovering a public parking lot by the Mississippi River on Broadway Street. I parked, then strolled along a walking path, known as the Natchez Trail, towards a gazebo at Bluff Park, overlooking the Mighty Mississippi River. The trail was a combination of city streets and walkways with painted panels depicting the history of the area. I had researched and found it was the best place to observe a sunset. I noticed others wandering down a steep hill. At the base was the section known as "Under the Hill". The location was exploited in the movie *Life* with Eddie Murphy and Martin Lawrence. It was a lot smaller than I anticipated, with only a small number of establishments to drink a beer or eat. An appealing locality was Mark Twain's guest house. It was a three-room house with a shared bathroom.

The weather was relatively toasty for March, in the mid-80s. I retreated up the steep slope after a quick visit to Under the Hill. The combination of the hill and humidity generated a sweat. Walking further, I came across Main Street. I arrived at an outdoors store, Bowie Outfitter, and asked about safe locations to bed down inside the truck. They said the perfect locale was the State Park. I knew the goal was to allocate money for a hotel/campground only about once a week. I continued walking Main Street, pausing at a shop. The owner was sweeping their outside entrance. I asked her about street performing and busking. She peered at me as if I was cuckoo. I took it as a no.

I retreated to the truck to reassess the situation. Natchez, Mississippi had a casino, the Magnolia Bluffs Casino. I went to investigate it. My oldest brother, John, had been homeless for two months. He had positioned himself in a casino parking lot, and he had expressed how safe he was there. The Magnolia Bluffs Casino in Natchez was designed to resemble the old Learned Saw Mill. The location was directly on the banks of the Mississippi River. I noticed they had security cameras under the different levels of covered parking. Fortunately, there were no cameras on the roof top. I thought the cameras would be a problem, so I parked on the exposed roof top. I walked inside to examine the casino and its amenities. It was predominantly slot machines with a few craps and blackjack tables. They had a miniature poker room closed for an undetermined amount of time. The most important thing I wanted were the bathrooms. The plan of sleeping in the truck meant using restrooms for shaving, brushing teeth, and changing clothes. They had one unisex bathroom for the entire casino. I decided it was not practical. I departed the Casino and returned to the public parking lot along the Mississippi River. Luckily, there was some construction taking place, and they had a Porta-John. The inside was clean, so the idea of spending the night in the parking lot seemed more appealing. I had a public area with lights and a bathroom if needed. I possessed water for shaving and brushing my teeth. I had food to prepare for dinner. Besides, I could view the sunset over the Mississippi River.

As I parked next to the river, I recalled Quarter Love, a Facebook friend who lived in Natchez. I had never engaged with her in person before, although we shared a lot of mutual friends. She was a music promoter in the area. I blindly issued her a Facebook message explaining who I was and what I was working on. About twenty minutes later, I received a text from her. She invited me out to connect with her and friends at Bowie's Tavern. Unknown to me, she had contrived arrangements with Kevin, a friend of hers hosting the karaoke night at the tavern, to enable me to perform a song or two between people desiring to sing karaoke. We established a bond quickly. We discussed music and her dream of becoming a full-time music promoter. I perceived a chemistry of attraction. The conversation at times was flirtatious. She had a beautiful smile. Besides, we were similar, pursuing our dreams one baby step at a time because it was what our heart was telling us to do. She introduced me to her friends and offered a location to sleep for two nights. She owned a home built in the 1800s, which she was remodeling for a future bed-and-breakfast. It allowed me to remain in town to enjoy St. Patty's Day and attend a performance of a band she had booked at a local venue.

Quarter Love also provided the number of an establishment in Natchez which might book me for a paying gig. The evening progressed, and I performed a song or two between others singing karaoke. Unfortunately, Bowie's only had about 6 people in it, besides our small group of people, so the prospect of selling autographed *Crossroads* EPs was bleak.

I connected with some interesting and creative people, including a guy who was a lead singer in a local band. He shared stories about performing in the Natchez area, explaining how one night the band's audience would be almost 300 people and the next night only ten people.

Karaoke wrapped up, and Kevin, the host, purchased an EP and collected my contact information. He said he would share my music around the Natchez area. Perhaps it could open a few doors of opportunity when I returned from my tour. My friend, Quarter Love, said she could book me at a location in Vicksburg, Mississippi.

MARCH 16, 2016

It was the first day, and things were starting to manifest promisingly on the music front.

I was invited to join everyone at the Under the Hill Saloon. The Saloon was originally built in the late 1700s. It had a history of being a brothel, a warehouse, general store, and of course a bar. The bar contained about 50 people milling around with a band providing live music. We stayed there for a few hours talking, laughing, and flirting. I connected with a guy named Jean Lue; he told me about two locales which might grant me permission to perform on the streets the next day. He stated there was a riverboat docked in front of the Under the Hill Saloon tomorrow. He believed the owner would gladly allow me to perform inside or outside for a few hours. He mentioned a coffee house, Steampunk Coffee Roasters, located on High Street, which might permit me to perform. They were located on the parade route for the St. Patrick's Day Parade taking place the next day.

I was finally feeling fatigued, so Quarter Love led me to the house she was letting me stay at for a couple of nights free of charge. As I followed her to the house, I received a phone call from Kevin. I had accidentally forgotten my iPad. It was on the top of his equipment. He called to arrange a location to link up so he could return it. I was overwhelmed with gratitude. I thought I had packed it before I left the tavern. As we arrived at the house, I told Quarter Love about the error with the iPad. I told her I needed to return to the Under the Hill

Saloon to connect with Kevin. She understood, but first she wanted to show me the inside of her home, as she would be returning to her friends at the Under the Hill Saloon then to her home afterwards.

It was a traditional Victorian home constructed in the 1800s, two blocks from Main Street. The interior had period furniture from the era as well. Each step the wooden hardwood floors creaked. The kitchen had the necessities to prepare simple meals as the construction was taking place. The laundry room had a working washer and dryer. The spiraling staircase to the second floor formed an image of horror movies, dark with multiple closed doors. The room she had chosen for me was one with its own bathroom. There were other rooms which I considered visiting later in the evening. I returned to the kitchen, where Quarter Love was leaning against the counter. I could not resist, and I kissed her. With completion of a brief kiss, we returned to the Under the Hill Saloon so I could meet Kevin.

After retrieving the iPad, I paused at the public parking lot by the Mississippi River. I parked by the river repeating positive affirmations, *"It's possible, I was successful, I believed, I had unwavering faith, etc."* A multitude of fears and doubts crept into my mind, even at this early stage of the tour. With all the lucky breaks I'd had on the first day, I knew I couldn't allow the doubts to overcome me. The dreams I had pushed me forward like the powerful current of the Mississippi River. I perceived my dreams were just on the horizon. Only one more curve or one extra bend, there would be the treasure I seek. I trusted in myself, and I trusted God. I told myself, *"I am persistent. I continue to have inspiration and faith."* Soon, those positive beliefs overcame the fleeting moment of weakness; I sensed harmony.

Day One of the remarkable journey was in the books. I could not have asked for anything more. I'd made it to Natchez, Mississippi safely. I had interacted with intriguing people who admired what I was accomplishing. I was given a free place to crash for two nights. I had sold one autographed EP of *Crossroads*. I was truly blessed and grateful.

The one big thing I'd forgotten was to eat dinner. Trying to conserve money, I dropped by a grocery store and purchased food in Pearl. But with everything falling into place so quickly, I never had an opportunity to prepare anything to eat. At the tavern, I avoided the menu and consumed alcohol only, two beers. When I did not eat regularly, I suffered from migraines. As the clock hit 1:30 a.m. I endured the pain of a migraine pounding behind my eyes. So, I assembled a sandwich, ingested medicine, and trusted it would bring prompt relief before the migraine became too severe. I returned to the upstairs bedroom anticipating sleep in a dark quiet room to remove the migraine.

Instead, reclined in bed, I experienced a surge of energy. I stayed awake until 4:00 a.m. or so. My mind began to yearn to figure out time to practice the guitar daily. Not only to learn cover songs and build playlists, or memorize lyrics, but to execute exercises to improve my skills. In addition, I wanted to establish time daily to read works by the people who inspired me, such as Paulo Coelho and Dan Millman, along with the YouTube channels. I desired to compose insights about each day in my journal while thoughts were still fresh. I knew I must create a plan including a schedule allowing me to consistently complete these important tasks.

Finally, I had thoughts of what tomorrow might hold. Eventually, I slipped into sleep.

The American Queen Steamboat
Docked at the Under the Hill Saloon

CHAPTER 7

MARCH 17, 2016

I awakened slowly. I had not fallen asleep until the wee hours of the morning. I lounged in bed until 9:00 a.m. The mattress embraced my body, along with the warm and cozy blankets. My mind and body advised me to sleep a little longer. However, I knew the importance of launching into the day.

The first item on the agenda was to partake of breakfast. It had been almost 24 hours since my last significant meal. Oddly, I was not starving. On the other hand, I knew I had to eat. Regular consumption of food controlled my migraines. I had a few basic staples in the truck: apples, cashews, almonds, protein mix, and bananas. Instead, I chose to find a restaurant. I departed the house and the historic district of Natchez in search of a diner or Waffle House. After driving about 10 minutes, I came across a

Shoney's restaurant and decided it was a good day for a breakfast buffet.

As always, my eyes were grander than my stomach. The buffet possessed everything a country boy desired: scrambled eggs, bacon, sausage, pancakes, plus fruit and multiple types of donuts. I scarfed down two plates of food rapidly. My stomach pooched out; I was nauseated. It triggered a cough and suddenly I found myself in the bathroom, vomiting my breakfast. This had happened in the past. In 2012, while I was on pilgrimage in France and Spain on the Camino de Santiago ("A Country Boy on the Camino"). It happened twice. I would have a meal, and within about five minutes, vomit. Then 10 minutes after, I was dandy, as if nothing had ever happened.

After leaving the restaurant, I traveled to the Under the Hill district of Natchez. I was informed the previous evening the Steamboat American Queen would be docked there. It was a prime opportunity to busk on the street. I was delighted as it was my first time ever street performing. It was the underlying mission of the tour. I requested permission to busk from the Under the Hill Saloon along with the Silver Street Gallery & Gifts next door. Both establishments granted me permission to perform. I situated myself across the street from the steamboat, to the right of the Silver Street Gallery & Gifts.

Employing the battery-powered amp for the first time since I had purchased it, I began performing. Nearly all the passengers strolled the boat side of the street. There were the taxis they needed to explore Natchez. Several people gazed over and smiled from time to time. A few travelers sat outside of the Under the Hill Saloon about fifty yards away, indulging in a beer or two. The weather was surprisingly warmer than I had anticipated. I continued busking. A few people approached and donated a few dollars in the tip jar. Near the end of the performance, a gentleman came over and purchased a copy of my autographed EP. I performed for roughly an hour and a half.

An additional goal of busking, besides earning tips to eat, was to develop enhanced eye contact with people. I wanted to draw them in as I performed. I noticed when holding eye contact, I generated a smile in addition to higher attention. Securing their attention usually meant an improved performance, which produced a boosted opportunity for tips along with EP sales. To retain eye contact, I had to memorize the lyrics of songs I performed. I struggled recalling lyrics by memory. Even with the originals I composed, I used my iPad as a safety net.

I suffered a few errors throughout the street performance. I sang the incorrect line or strummed an improper chord, no doubt due to a bit of nervousness. I wanted to eliminate those mistakes, to polish the act to prepare for future paying gigs.

As the trip progressed, I further understood the urgency to have time to practice and master other cover songs. My current repertoire only consisted of 35 songs, whereas I had friends who possessed over 200.

I collected the equipment and retreated to the house Quarter Love was allowing me to stay in. I was spoiled in Natchez. I had been given a home to occupy for free, had interacted with lovely people, and street-performed the first time in my life. It was what I had dreamed the tour to be each day across America.

Although I was not squandering time watching TV, the day passed surprisingly quickly. Around 4:00 p.m. I set off to purchase two bags of ice for the plastic cooler. The bag I'd acquired the day before had already melted. I invested in an economical cooler, "cheap". The ice melted in about a day with the combination of heat of the outside temperatures plus being locked away inside the locked truck bed cover. Not good since I had milk, eggs and lunch meat inside the cooler. I mulled over procuring a Yeti cooler. It would have been a wiser decision instead of the inexpensive plastic one. During the errand, I planned to deliver a booking kit to the venue which Quarter Love mentioned the initial evening in Natchez. Unfortunately, after the ice purchase, those plans changed. A thunderstorm rolled into town like a runaway freight train. Within five minutes, a cloudburst spawned a torrential rain obscuring my vision. The wind growled and swirled, toppling trees along with launching people's garbage cans down the street. Hail plummeted from the blackened skies. Luckily it was comparable only to miniature golf balls. I parked 50 yards from the Mississippi River. The downpour vanished the river like a Las Vegas Illusionist. The roadways surged with debris. As the parking lot transitioned into a lagoon, I decided it was most fitting to return to the house and wait out the storm.

An hour later, the rainstorm persisted. The outside temperature had dropped 20 degrees. I had aimed to busk at the coffee shop during the afternoon ahead of the St. Patrick's Day parade starting at 6:30 p.m. Sadly, the storm made it impossible.

I had been invited to a party later in the night after the parade by Quarter Love. She was a music promoter for Smoot's Grocery on Broadway street, approximately five blocks away from the house. It was St. Patrick's Day, and she had booked an Irish band to perform. I was contemplating walking, but considering the dreadful weather, I drove. Unfortunately, the parade on Main Street was canceled.

I arrived at Smoot's Grocery at dusk. The rain had halted; a true blessing. The building was originally built in 1939. Its claim to fame was the Mississippi Blues. Nearly all the finest Blues Men of Mississippi had performed there at some point or another. The outside of Smoot's reminded me of an old country store…the distressed wooden outer walls with its rust-covered tin roof along with advertising placards. The inside opened into a large room filled with sofas, plush chairs and tables with a main stage. Because of St. Patrick's Day, they grilled sausages and cabbage with a plethora of green beer.

The Irish band rocked the evening away. Patrons fashioned in St. Patrick's Day garb spun and swayed and boozed away. Out of nowhere, a line of bag pipers horned into the bar and mingled with the celebration.

The clock struck midnight. I cruised to the Victorian home, drowsy. The earlier rain disturbance had chilled the house. I shrouded myself with a long-sleeved shirt and clambered into bed. As I lounged in bed, I cherished the intimacy of the blankets and pillows. I burrowed under those blankets and contemplated. Two days had elapsed swiftly. I imagined at daybreak I'd be on the road elsewhere, uttering farewell to Natchez, The "Confessions of a Dreamer Tour" moving onward. Natchez was blissful. I was genuinely grateful to Quarter Love for helping a dreamer perform the night before and providing a free location to sleep for a couple of nights. I had connected with delightful people. Everyone was extremely kind, loving, and supportive. I recited prayers of thanks for them and sent them my best wishes.

Most evenings before I slumbered, I said affirmations which I had attained from the previously mentioned authors I studied or the YouTube channels I listened to. *"I have faith all will be good. When I want something, the universe conspires in my favor, I know this. I feel it, I sense it, and I believe it is already here. I just relax, let it go and have no doubts. I am remaining positive, happy, and joyous. I have the courage to look into the dark places of my soul to ensure I am not asking for the wrong things."* I prayed the remaining tour would progress favorably as I drifted off to sleep.

A distant clatter awakened me, producing a startled sensation. I gazed over at the alarm clock. It read 3:30 a.m. I calmly left the bed and walked to the entry of the bedroom. My hand clenched the 9mm handgun. Someone was keying the lock downstairs. I seized my cell phone. Unfortunately, it displayed no bars of service. My breath quickened. My muscles tensed. The door from below opened. Thankfully a voice confirmed it was Quarter Love. I exhaled a deep breath. Come to find out the earlier storm had knocked out her power. She was spending the evening downstairs in a bedroom. As I heard her lock the door, I ascended the stairs with those creaky wooden floors and crawled into bed. I sat in silence and asked myself: was I truly prepared for the tour? *I was trusting my intuition. I had committed to the dreams I had been writing about in my journal. I had faith I could become my higher self. I trusted doorways would be opened.* I drifted off to sleep again.

The Mississippi River
Taken from the Magnolia Bluffs Casino

CHAPTER 8

MARCH 18, 2016

I awakened to a thunderstorm. I had planned to depart to travel west. Regrettably, the continued thunderstorms postponed the departure. So, instead of pursuing an early start, I remained snuggled under blankets.

An hour went by. I overheard my friend Quarter Love downstairs. I descended the stairs and entered the kitchen. She asked me to hang out with her before I left. She invited me to her favorite restaurant, Nikki's Family Restaurant. It was located over the Natchez-Vidalia Bridge, across the Louisiana state line. It was adorned with memorabilia from different stages of its history. It had operated since 1983.

Entering the restaurant, the aroma of country-prepared cuisine flashed me back to my Granny's house in Zama, Mississippi. The Southern meal consisted of jambalaya, green beans, yams, fried okra, fried catfish, hushpuppies, and cornbread. It was buffet style, all you could eat. I decided on only one plate to avoid becoming sick like the day before. One plate was chosen, but trust me, it was a mountain of Southern delights. Southern food was delicious and was my all-time favorite no matter how detrimental it might be for the heart and the love handles. The food was amazing. The flavors burst in my mouth and tantalized my taste buds.

After our meal, Quarter Love and I proceeded to the Under the Hill Saloon. We conversed with some locals sitting at the bar. I spoke with the bartender, describing my dream along with the tour. He said he had recently returned from a motorcycle trip to Colorado. Not long before, he had toured Oregon and Washington State. He was in preparation to cruise through Canada within the next few months. I immediately thought of him as a kindred spirit.

Suddenly, I realized a delightful aspect of the tour was connecting with people who were normally outside my social circle on account of my being too afraid to talk to them due to their outward appearance. It was one of the main reasons I cherished traveling. It shattered barriers and heralded new, interesting people into my life.

After leaving the Under the Hill Saloon with Quarter Love, I returned to the house for a snooze. After I awakened, I arranged the truck for tomorrow's departure.

MARCH 18, 2016

I debated a bike ride to locate a place to perform music. But, the storms drifted in with hard rain, roaring thunder, and risky lightning. Though only 5:00 p.m., the elements had brought ominous skies comparable to the darkness of nightfall. I discovered yesterday's storm had been remarkably punishing. It ripped sections of the American Queen Steamboat's roof off. The rainstorm endured.

I used the remainder of the day to wrap up emails and social media. I wanted to accomplish a lot each day in multiple areas. It was an ambitious plan; possibly a downfall. I had been instructed, "to master something, you need to discipline yourself to practice it at least four hours a day, six days a week for about seven years." With the present strategy I employed, I might remain satisfactory at multiple things, but not ever become great at any of them.

The thunderstorms showed no signs of stopping. It was definitely a further hindrance to a live performance. I chose to take advantage of the dreadful weather to do laundry and try to compose lyrics. I did not have a phone signal inside the house where I was staying. There was no WiFi, cable or a TV. So, it was just me, entertained by the patter of rain on the roof of an 1800s home. It was a peaceful harmony conducive to work. It removed many of the most common modern distractions, and, fortunately, the roof was impermeable.

The rainstorm at last ceased. It allowed an evening to celebrate my final night in Natchez. I returned to the Under the Hill Saloon, understanding there was a cover charge of $5. The Saloon had a live band beginning at 9:00 p.m. I perched on a bar stool for about an hour, drinking a cold beer and listening to the band play Southern rock. There were not many people inside, perhaps due to the weather or perhaps they showed at a much later time as it was only about 10:30 p.m. After finishing the beer, I decided it was time to retire to the house and call it a quiet night.

Back at the house, I folded the laundry and prepared things for my departure the next morning. I reviewed the road atlas and considered different possible routes into Texas. Houston was the next location, where I had a friend and a few open mic possibilities. I was bypassing San Antonio, as they did not allow street busking. My other objective was to only travel on backroads and stay away from the Interstates, so I could truly see America.

As I laid in bed, I contemplated the daily readings which maintained my purpose and faith. I achieved wisdom from many different sources: YouTube videos, books, along with inspirational emails I received daily, like Tiny Buddha.

I was chasing dreams. I had faith and trust in God my instincts would show me my way. What I sought was seeking me. I already had it. I just needed to relax and let it go. I believed God would open the doors for me. I knew if I was not taking this trip, I would have had regrets. Regrets could kill, they slowly ate away at your soul. I was taking full responsibility for everything I did. Hope saw the invisible, felt the intangible, and achieved the impossible. I was courageous. I carried in my memory the good things which had come out of past difficulties. They served as proof of my abilities and gave me confidence when I faced obstacles. Everything and anything was possible. I was not afraid to dream big. I had patience. Everything in life had its price. There was nothing to hold me back except myself. Everything I encountered was only a step along the way to my dreams. I had decided what I wanted. I believed I could have it. I believed I deserved it. I believed it was possible for me.

El Camino East/West Corridor
"The King's Highway"

CHAPTER 9

MARCH 19, 2016

I decided each day of the tour I'd drive for about four to five hours. Overall, I thought it would be a desirable goal. It allowed time to arrive in a city, busk on the streets, time to locate a venue to perform at an open mic, as well as locate a safe place I could sleep for the night.

Departing Natchez, I remained on the road less traveled. I crossed the Mississippi River driving west on Highway 84. It was mostly two-lane blacktops. The one major problem I detected was due to the heavy rains over the past few days, flooding had occurred. The bayous were cresting over their banks. Unfortunately, many homes which I passed were flooded. I witnessed a pickup truck with water up to its roof.

I arrived at the Dewey Wills Wildlife Management region and decided to proceed forward to Alexandria,

Louisiana. In Alexandria, I contemplated transitioning to the interstate, I-49 west. On second thought, I remained on the country roads to observe America at a slower pace. I transitioned onto Highway 28 West. It directed me over the Kincaid Reservoir. It seemed like a great place for the surrounding areas to enjoy numerous forms of recreation. The final miles of Louisiana were spent on Highway 63 West. It dissected the Clear Creek Wildlife Management Area. Those rural areas offered multiple locations to camp inside of my truck, but, nowhere to perform. The keen feature about the day's trip through Louisiana were the signs displaying "El Camino." As I have mentioned before, in 2012 I walked the Camino de Santiago from France to Spain. I completed over 600 miles walking in the footsteps of St. James over 40 days. I wrote about the adventure in my first E-book, "A Country Boy on the Camino." I perceived the presence of God's guiding hand with those signs.

As I advanced, I contemplated sites to stop and sleep. I was researching free or cheap camping sites on the web using my smartphone. The website www.freecampsites.net stated: "Whether you just need to know where to camp nearby or you want to plan a free camping road trip, we've got you covered. You can simply use your smart phone's GPS to find camping near you or even use our trip planner to plan your route from coast to coast. Our community provides the best free camping information available." I noted a few public parks attached to the

Wildlife Management areas and the Anacoco Lake, but I assumed they were only open during the daytime so I forged ahead.

As I moved across the Texas State line. The first thing I noticed was the speed limit. It increased to 75 miles per hour. I pushed on until I arrived in Lufkin, Texas. Upon my arrival, I commenced what would become the daily ritual. I arrived in a city from the day's travels. I attempted to locate a venue or popular street area to perform. If I were not able to perform, I would search out a Starbucks to take advantage of their free WiFi. I could manage social media responsibilities, write in my journal, and handle phone calls. Then finally, locate a safe spot to sleep inside the truck.

It was late afternoon when I arrived in Lufkin. I briefly ventured around the city before locating the nearest Starbucks. I had read Lufkin was founded in 1882. It had a population of over 40,000 people. An interesting observation I made while driving: the city had lovely murals painted by an artist named Lance Hunter throughout the downtown area.

Inside the Starbucks, I located a deserted chair near an electrical outlet where I could start the duties of social media announcements, charging devices, and writing inside my journal. I indulged in a steaming cupful of green tea. The aroma was a jasmine blend. I had to sample the tea cautiously due to its temperature. I savored the tea for an hour. When I had finished the above tasks at Starbucks, I located a nearby Wal-Mart and explored the lot for a parking space. I wanted a location near a security light but not too distant from the store.

I was fairly sleepy after the lengthy day of driving. So, with the sun hovering above, I tested the backseat bed for the first time. Though it was chilly outside, the truck interior was quite warm. I had two guitars stacked up behind the seats blocking a direct view of the backseat from the windshield perspective. I draped a jacket on a hanger by the back driver's-side window and the same on the passenger's back window. I covered the back window with hanging shirts to create a secluded cave. To enter into the den, I had to go from the back doors of the pick-up truck. Before I snuggled into my nest, I surveyed the people around. I wanted to slip in so no one knew what I was doing.

The backseat offered minimal padding. I would advise others to create an increased plush bunk. Though I was five feet six inches, I had to curl like a baby to fit properly. I noticed it was difficult to change positions as well. I probably slept almost an hour. What with the sounds of cars cruising around and it being the first time I tried to sleep like this, I was unable to relax. It felt like someone might be looking in on me, considering whether the Wal-Mart camping idea might be more difficult for me than I had originally thought. I dispatched a couch surfing request and thought about finding a free campsite. I received no response to the email, and the free campsite was about a 45-minute drive away.

MARCH 19, 2016

I retreated to the Starbucks from earlier. I repeated the prior steps. I observed people coming and going and wondered what their life might be like. Were these individuals living the life of their dreams or walking blindly through the motions? The Starbucks remained open until midnight. I decided to linger there until it turned dark then make my way back to the Wal-Mart parking lot to sleep for the night. I planned to head into Houston, TX the next day.

I located another space comparable to the one from before. The cooler temperatures concerned me, because I was worried I would become chilly at night sleeping in the back seat of my truck. I went inside the Wal-Mart to use the bathroom to brush my teeth. I had learned to say I was not nervous, but excited. Excitement and nervousness produced the same symptoms in our bodies. But as I strolled through the store, I leaned to the term "nervousness." I had never employed a Wal-Mart as my bathroom in this nature. I walked around the entire Super Wal-Mart before entering the bathroom. Luckily, it was empty. I brushed and flossed my teeth and exited. I returned to my truck with the toothbrush and supplies in my pockets.

At the truck, I crawled into the backseat, kicking my shoes onto the floor. I ensured I could easily reach the 9mm handgun in case of emergency. I rustled around to locate a comfortable position. I placed the eye cover on to block out the security light and closed my eyes.

The goal for the next day was to pinpoint a location to busk or an open mic to perform. It would be Sunday, so I would have to see if things were open and available.

The nightly routine of saying positive affirmations launched. *I was so grateful I could do this. Ask, believe, and have faith with expectations to receive it. I knew God knew perfectly well what was best for me. He would continue to do as He saw fit. I allowed my life to develop according to my Creator's plans. I was brave. I had courage. God had prepared a path for me to follow. I just had to have faith and follow the signs He had left for me. I was following my dreams through to their conclusions. I sensed God wanted me to be successful. God would lead me.*

I was inspired by Jim Rohn to take risks, to pursue goals, to accomplish my plan. Life might feel like a rollercoaster. Life was never smooth. It could have many bumps along the way.

I said, "let's make today our best day." Do not fret about yesterday or have anxiety about tomorrow. Live for today, be present.

> *"To attain his dream, he needed a strong will and an enormous capacity for acceptance. Although he might have an objective, the path leading to the objective was not always as he imagined it would be."*
> *–Paulo Coelho*

Hermann Park
Houston, Texas

CHAPTER 10

MARCH 20, 2016

Last night was the inaugural night for sleeping in the truck. I had hit the sack around 10:00 p.m. after experimenting with various arrangements to be as comfortable as possible. I wanted to eliminate as much movement as I could so not to alert the public I was sleeping in the truck. I was safe; I was in a Wal-Mart parking lot about 200 yards away from the RVs and tractor trailer trucks camping for the evening.

The truck's back seat was constricted. I had to rest in a curled position the entire time. I reminded myself of a sleeping infant tucked away in blankets. The outside temperature dropped into the low 40s, so I became a bit cold. I used a sleeping bag as a blanket. As the temperatures decreased, I added clothing. In case the temperatures were ever to approach freezing, I had packed my deer hunting apparel for warmth.

The worst thing was having to use the bathroom in the middle of the night. I was parked about four football fields away from the entrance. So, the idea of having to walk into the Wal-Mart around 1:00 a.m. to use their bathroom in 40-degree weather was not enticing. Still, I concluded it was the most desirable option. I was amazed when I entered the store at 1:00 a.m. at the volume of people who were there shopping. Some families even had their small children with them. I was an observer. I was a people watcher. My late-night obligation provided me with the perfect opportunity to indulge the interest. The main feature jumping out was the considerable amount of obese people and smokers I witnessed. It created an opinion. Here I was chasing my dreams. I had given up everything comfortable and familiar in life to be able to do this. Yet as I looked around at all the people who were obviously not taking very good care of themselves, I couldn't help but wonder: did they ever dream? If so, at what point did they give up on their dreams to slide down onto their current paths? I was not saying I was better or worse than the people I noticed, just curious about how they got there.

When I awoke in the morning around 7:00 a.m. I decided to experiment with a bottle in the truck to urinate into instead of making the long walk into the cold to the Wal-Mart bathroom. Besides, the truck was started, with the heater on high. While the interior became toasty, I did not want to venture into the cold environment. So, I did the best I could not to let anyone see what I was doing. I used an old Gatorade bottle with a large opening to ensure no spillage occurred.

After I warmed up, I moved the truck closer to the Wal-Mart entrance. There was a McDonalds inside, so I ate a small breakfast and then proceeded to the restroom to brush my teeth. I purchased a few small items and returned to the truck.

I pondered visiting a local park in Lufkin which offered mountain bike trails. Unfortunately, it was too cold outside. Instead, I decided it was best to proceed to Houston.

Roughly 45 minutes outside of Lufkin, I paused at a small picnic area and changed clothes. While there, I attempted to rearrange some items inside the truck to create a more comfortable back seat. I rearranged the guitar cases, increasing seclusion from the front windshield as well as allowing more space for my feet. It worked a little; however, I still needed to remain curled up, which led to some bilateral knee discomfort.

I left the park, but after an hour or so of driving, I became drowsy. I located a Love's truck stop on the map in Cleveland, Texas. I came across a parking spot not too far away from the entrance to not invite suspicion, but not too close to be filled with distractions. I once again climbed into the back and took a nap.

When I awoke, I chose to use their facilities. Truck stops were a helpful commodity. They were normally open 24 hours, offered restrooms, WiFi, and showers. Inside were usually a restaurant and even a game room if one was bored. While at the Love's truck stop, I received an email message from a gentleman who lived in Houston. When researching Houston about busking, I had contacted a few individuals whom I had located on ReverbNation. He had found through research street busking was illegal there. I had previously read some threads from 2015 stating people could perform on the street in certain areas. I would not know what was true until I arrived in Houston and asked around and attempted some busking to see what would happen.

I was curious to learn if Houston had any 24-hour Fitness Centers. If yes, I could visit it in the Houston area. I was hoping they had showers. It would be nice to work out and then take a long, hot shower.

I had created a couch surfing profile and emailed a request for the Houston area. Sadly, I had not yet heard anything back.

It was a little after noon when I departed the truck stop. I guessed it was time to get energetic and reach Houston. During the drive into Houston, the engine light of the truck illuminated. It meant I needed an oil change soon. It was something I had neglected before the initial departure in Mississippi. I knew I would have to tackle the maintenance before I drove too far.

I was on I-69 south into Houston. The interstate created a dazing effect. My mind began to wander. Sometimes when I was watching other people, my mind created doubt and fear. *Should I return to orthopedic surgery as a physician assistant? It was safe. I would have a stable income, be able to accomplish some things.* Then I pondered what could happen when dreams became reality. *The desires of travel, writing, composing, and performing all over the world was what kept me moving forward and aiming so high. My dreams allowed me to discover liberties I could only imagine.* "Dream big," I continued declaring to myself. "Live life like you can't fail. All things were possible!"

I arrived in Houston, Texas in the early afternoon. I initially drove to an area called Rice Village. When I arrived at Rice Village, I found it was primarily a strip mall with high-end stores. There was not a quad or plaza where people would be sitting around or passing through. Instead of attempting a street busk, I located a 24-Hour Fitness where I chose to work out. I had not exercised in over two weeks due to the planning and moving out. After my workout, I did the best to clean up in the bathroom, as they did not have a shower. I had purchased outdoor cleaning tissue wraps at Wal-Mart, and I used them. I could at least sponge off my body. I had also invested in dry shampoo for my hair.

Next, I located a Starbucks. I used the time to complete social media activities. I conducted an internet search for open mics in the Houston area. Fortunately, I discovered an open mic I could perform at the following night.

As the Starbucks visit went on, I discovered I had a high school friend at the nearby airport. She was a flight attendant. She was on stand-by for a flight to North Carolina, our childhood home. I contacted her through Facebook messenger. She said if she did not get on a flight, she would be staying overnight in Houston. If that occurred, I could see her and catch up. It had been over 20 years since I had seen her last. Approximately thirty minutes later, she texted me a flight was available. In a brief moment, the sensation of excitement turned to disappointment. I rebounded from the news, though, and redirected my attention to locate a business for truck service. A handful of places emerged from Yelp. I decided to take the truck the next day for service to avoid any damage from not changing the oil. The truck was my home for another six weeks. I needed it to function properly. I did not want to become stranded on the roadside at any point along the tour.

Since my arrival in Houston, I had not yet explored the downtown area. I had been traveling the outskirts of the city locating items I desired. Primarily, those were locations like a gym and the Starbucks.

I was finishing up the Starbucks break while pondering the requirement of finding a safe spot to sleep. The person I contacted on Couch Surfing earlier had not responded to my email. It appeared a Wal-Mart evening was most likely. I located a couple of Wal-Marts in the area. I exited the Starbucks to visit each one to confirm it was safe and open 24-hours.

As I was driving around those new locations, I declared to myself: *These are not strange, just new to me. Besides, this was what I chose to do, to understand and see new places. I am an adventurer on a quest arising from my dreams. I have faith.* I remained relaxed and unhurried. Patience was the key. I sustained the sentiment that I was making the correct decision. I understood doubts and fears were trying to interrupt me. I had petitioned clearly what it was I sought. God was with me. I was confident. When anxiety, despair, and worry crept into my mind, I dismissed them with positive, optimistic thoughts of success.

I say listen to your heart. Have the courage to embrace your deepest desires. Be true to yourself. Each day we are given 24-hours. Do your best to utilize it wisely.

Maintain your will power. Be determined to yearn for everything you would like to see happen in your life. A YouTube channel called *Absolute Motivation* posted a video saying, "It's up to you, every passing moment is another chance to turn it all around."

I have faith you will transform yourself into what you desire the most. I trust you are extraordinary.

Sam Houston Horse Statue Arch
Hermann Park
Houston, Texas

CHAPTER 11
MARCH 21, 2016

To sleep the night before, I had chosen another Wal-Mart parking lot. I traveled initially to one location, but I did not fancy the environment of it. The parking lot was cramped, with limited security lights. I viewed four police cars parked in the vicinity providing more negative vibes. I trusted my instincts. Instead, I located a different Wal-Mart. The new parking lot had a few campers and large tractor trailers amid the spaces. There was ample security lighting as well. I strolled inside around 11:30 p.m. Once again there were families shopping with little children.

It was a crisp night in Houston with the temperatures descending into the low 40s. I slept well. I remained in the fetal position without tossing and turning. My knees did not ache in the morning. I entered the Wal-Mart after I awoke, to brush my teeth and use the restroom, and I decided on a McDonald's hot breakfast. The food staples in the truck consisted of cashews, almonds, and an apple. The colder temperatures created a desire for a hot sausage biscuit, hash browns, and orange juice instead. Back at the truck, I dressed in clean clothes and typed the auto repair shop into Google maps.

Google maps guided me to the auto repair shop I had found on Yelp in the museum district. The shop was called Midtown Auto Repair. The owner, Mon Yu, was professional and friendly. I required the 120,000-mile check-up. To complete the service, quite a few tasks were needed. Originally, the charge was over $500. Obviously, the price was not in the original planned budget. After chatting about how the truck was performing, he modified the service. He also subtracted $50 off the service invoice for completing a review on Yelp and Google. He noticed the mountain bike attached to the truck. He stated he was an avid bike rider. He biked from Houston to Austin (165 miles) yearly as a member of a local charity. He described how Houston was an excellent location for all biking, on- and off-road.

He noted the Mississippi driver's license and asked what had brought me to Houston. I shared the trip's details. I stated my desire to chase my dreams, listen to my heart, and trust my instincts. I sensed I may have inspired him some. He voiced, even though he owned the shop and did very well financially, that his heart was into local mission work. He helped the homeless of the Houston area with the assistance of his church. They offered meals and encouraging words along with protection from the elements with blankets when possible.

Mon Yu said the museum district was close to his shop and while he repaired the truck, I should utilize my bike to see it. I agreed, as traveling by bicycle was easier than an automobile in cities. So, while the truck was serviced, I rode off on an adventure.

The district offered nineteen separate museums, walkable zones, and daily inspiration. Over the next two hours I progressed through the museum district. It was truly delightful and peaceful. It was a Monday. The streets were quiet with only a few people wandering the sidewalks. I rode around the Hermann Park. The park offered a Japanese Garden, the Miller Outdoor Theatre, and McGovern Lake. I locked my bike to a bench and walked into the Japanese Garden. It symbolized the friendship between the U.S. and Japan. Inside the garden, I located a statue of the great Confucius. The weather was sunny with clear blue Texas skies. I came upon the Houston Zoo and decided after the truck was finished, I would visit it.

I returned to the service shop and thanked Mon Yu for his assistance. I donated an autographed copy of my EP, *Crossroads*, along with a list of quotes which I used to remain motivated. I mentioned even baby steps towards a dream were a worthy goal. I stated my gratitude and shook his hand goodbye.

I had always enjoyed the zoo. Whenever I was visiting a new location, if they had a zoo, I would try to find the time to visit it. Overall I spent about three hours there. I observed the animals with high-rise office buildings in the background. It was a new twist for me, as the zoo was built inside the city. It offered more than 3,100 animals. Only a few attractions were closed; unfortunately, the rhino exhibit was one of them. The weather was favorable even in the middle of the day. Nearly all the animals were out and about in their zoo homes. I wondered what images were on the minds of animals being confined. Did they like it? Hate it? Or did they even understand the difference between freedom and being locked up for their entire lives?

I paused for a cold drink and decided to post on Facebook. I was blessed to discover a friend of mine from Florida who lived in Houston. She said I could drop by her place to shower before an open mic performance later in the evening. It was okay to visit and shower. Unluckily, she dwelled in a studio and her cousin was crashing on the sofa, which meant no room for me to sleep. She lived in a nifty loft apartment outside of the museum area.

The night before at the Starbucks, I had located an open mic at McGonigel's Mucky Duck. I arrived at McGonigel's at 7:00 p.m. I was surprised to see the list to perform was already filled out to 9:30 p.m. Regarding open mic nights, I never knew the best time to sign up on the list. It was my goal to perform in front of as many people as possible to spread my music, to gain more fans/followers, and to sell EPs. At some open mics, it was better to be one of the first performers, while at others it was prime to be near the end.

I waited at the bar sipping on a cold draft beer. I introduced myself to a couple of the other musicians and discussed what I was doing. Both said, "I want to do it too," so I offered them my contact information and told them to hit me up anytime. I truly believed I could be inspiring to others to follow their dreams and take risks for what they believed in. I was truly grateful and blessed.

Initially, McGonigel's was exactly what I wanted. It had an intimate atmosphere with a crowd there only to listen to music. The Mucky Duck possessed not a single TV. But as time progressed, more and more people arrived with different intentions. By the time I took the stage, the ambience had changed. It was like a large noisy bar or restaurant instead of a small music venue. The three tables directly by the stage were pushed together for a party of ten individuals with small children there for a dinner party to celebrate seeing each other. The noise they created was louder than the microphone. So, they were having their own party, which took away from the intimacy of the live music atmosphere. Afterwards, I spoke with the host of the open mic and he stated it was rare the atmosphere changed so quickly.

I once again made some mistakes while performing my original songs. Though I had composed them, I struggled to memorize my own lyrics. After the performance, I decided I had rushed through them too quickly. The lyrics were on an iPad which scrolled while I performed. I used a program called *Onsong*. During practice sessions, the timer aligned properly with my guitar and singing performance. Though, on the stage, I finished the song much earlier. I continued to up the tempo when performing live. The positive aspect of the night was successfully accomplishing my goal to become a storyteller as I performed. I could describe the significance behind each song. I incorporated my reasons for the current tour. Before I performed "Angel," I displayed the EP, *Crossroads*. I stated for a donation they could have one autographed. People applauded the story of my road trip, which lead into "Don't Look Back."

After I completed each song, the audience clapped, which was pleasant. The three-song set was finished. I remained for about another hour. Unfortunately, no one purchased an EP. Before I departed, I offered an autographed copy to a woman celebrating her birthday. We talked a bit. She stated one of her friends had family in Mississippi. I was seized by the beauty of the birthday girl. She was attractive, had no boyfriend or ring on her finger to indicate she was attached. I recounted my past career in orthopedic surgery, my book, "A Country Boy on the Camino," based on the Camino de Santiago, along with the reasons behind my current trip. She said she had done a walk in Peru. She was familiar with the

Camino de Santiago. She planned to complete the journey one day in the future. It was lovely connecting with her. Even early into the journey, the night was a major positive: improving my skills to connect with people. If I could improve either before I take the stage or while performing, I could become an improved performer. It was a tactic which lured people in during the performance. It created an amazing show and increased fans. I continued to practice with the goal of establishing a greater connection with my audiences.

I exited McGonigel's after 11 p.m. Before departing the parking lot, I contemplated. In my mind, I had the impression I was more experienced than most on the open mic stage. Nevertheless, after I performed, the inner voices of doubt entered. I overcame them with positive thoughts and faith. I had received emails and Facebook posts informing me how much people appreciated my lyrics and songs. This kept me going.

I located an IHOP. While waiting on my celebration big breakfast platter, I transcribed my thoughts about the evening. I addressed how proud I was of myself. I was dreaming big and performing tasks which eight months ago I did not knew existed. I was abolishing fear and learning to not care about what others expected. I was blessed, as well, with an outlet near the table, so I could charge my cell phone and iPad. I finished eating the scrambled eggs, sausage, pancakes, and hash browns. I realized I was quite exhausted so I decided not to perform my normal reading routine. I still had to find a safe location to sleep. I did an online search for a Wal-Mart, and luckily, a 24-hour Super Wal-Mart was convenient. Once there, I found a secure parking spot near a security light. A trick I had found was parking the passenger side of the truck next to a cart return area. This way, other cars could only park on the driver's side. My head was against the door on the passenger side. It offered a quieter scene. It was less likely someone would peek into the window. I curled inside the sleeping bag, thinking about the next day's goals. The plan was to arrive in Austin, Texas. I was usually awakened throughout the night due to noise. Fortunately, I was able to sleep straight until 9:00 a.m. The cold Houston night was not bothersome either. I sensed life wanted me to achieve my dreams.

Texas State Capitol Building
Austin, Texas

CHAPTER 12
MARCH 22, 2016

Last night had not been as chilly as the one before. When I awoke in the morning, I thought about the two individuals I connected with the previous night. They both had links with my home state of Mississippi. The gentleman had an association to Biloxi and Pascagoula. The woman I was introduced to was familiar with Philadelphia and the county I was born in, Attala.

I departed Houston for a two-and-a-half-hour drive to Austin, Texas. To persist with the original plans of driving mostly backroads, I selected TX-71-W instead of remaining on I-10-W until Austin. The trip passed through smaller towns and cities.

During the drive to Austin, I aimed to stop somewhere near La Grange, Texas for lunch. Despite having a road atlas, I could not locate the picnic area which the map had listed. I identified another location which supposedly offered everything I desired: privacy, picnic table, fire pit, view of nature, along with a view of the Colorado River. Yet, the spot was mislabeled as well. After I left the picnic area, I realized it was the original location listed on the map. Sadly, it was not located on the Colorado River as the map had shown.

I stopped by a few other places with picnic areas. However, most of them were state parks which charged an entrance fee. I completely understood why they charged fees, but for my needs, it was not worth paying money to sit at a table for only two hours knowing I could locate somewhere else to sit and eat for free.

Roughly twenty minutes outside of Austin, I stopped at a recreational public park to enjoy lunch. I was trying to consume my own food for as many meals per day as I could to save money. My usual breakfast consisted of peanut butter, cashews, almonds, and a piece of fruit. Lunch was a sandwich and chips with the cashews and almonds, as well as fruit. I possessed a butane camping stove to prepare hot meals, like soup, or to grill an item to eat.

There had been a large musical festival (SXSW) in Austin, Texas the previous week. I was arriving two days after it concluded. I was curious what the music scene in the city might look like. Would it keep rolling like it always did or would they pause to clean up, relax, and then kick everything back off as per usual?

I arrived in Austin. I had read it was a green city. Besides being the live music capitol of the world, it offered numerous outdoor activities. Austin came across as everyman's dream. I originally went to Zilkner Metropolitan Park. It was considered Austin's most-loved park. It was over 300 acres. I thought it would be a cool location to park and ride my bike into the city. Considering it was paid parking only, as well as too far from the downtown area, I instead continued driving until I located a free public parking lot near the Capitol building. Once parked, I mounted my bike to tour the city of Austin. I drifted for a few hours around the city. The pleasant sun caressed my face graciously. The temperature was in the low 70s, though an occasional strong wind gust made the bike unstable. I visited numerous downtown locations, such as the Capitol area on Upper Congress Avenue, Sixth Street, and Texas University. Two hours elapsed sight-seeing. I stopped in a small park to ponder the next move. I decided to conduct an internet search for locations to perform. I used the bike to observe those locations and to look for any other street performers. I found visiting a city on a bicycle was easier than a car. I had discovered when living in Philadelphia, Pennsylvania in 2002. I could use side streets, have no worries about parking, and cut across sidewalks. An added bonus was Austin extended a bicycle lane on all their streets downtown.

I persisted in the search for a street performer. I noticed no one. It was Wednesday afternoon. Perhaps busking was an evening activity in Austin. Maybe it's why I hadn't seen any street performers to date.

I saw a sign for a hostel. I recalled the Camino de Santiago trip. I had resided in Albergues which ranged from $5 – 20 dollars a night. I investigated the hostel. I asked the cost per night. I was amazed to find it was $35 for a room of six and $45 for a room of four per evening. I could stay in a Motel 6 for almost the same price and have a room all to myself. All the same, it mattered not: the hostel was full.

I left there, thinking from what I had read on the internet, a different street musician was performing on every corner in Austin. I spoke with a local shop owner who told me the city of Austin was attempting to restrict street performing. Recently, street performers were people basically beating on buckets. A few were okay, yet, when every street corner had them, it became a nuisance. Nonetheless, he instructed me to go for it. He mentioned some locations to try out. He added I should merely start performing and not ask permission. He insinuated the shop owners would decline my request. I was baffled because it was so different from the stories I had heard of Austin being a great live-music city, open to aspiring performers sharing their craft in public.

My stomach had become empty from the bike adventures. I decided to consume some of the BBQ Austin was famous for. I researched on Yelp to locate the best BBQ restaurant in the vicinity, rated by the locals. I spoke with a friend from Nashville. He jokingly told me to put out a sign stating, "I will busk for BBQ." I chose Franklin Barbecue, on 11th Street. I agreed with the ratings of cheap and excellent. As I consumed the meal, I thought about busking afterwards. Unfortunately, the mighty winds increased. They would have blown over the mic stand. I admitted I was deficient in self-confidence, though I had been pushing through fear since day one of the tour. I could easily allow myself not to perform a task due to fear and the thought of failure.

Instead, I returned to the public parking area. I racked the bike and located a Starbucks. Soon, I was sitting inside. I spent a few hours catching up on everything from the past few days. As I was writing, I dozed off. My head snapped up when I overheard myself snoring. I thought it would be excellent to stumble upon an interesting place to crash. It would be delightful to sit around a fire, relax, practice guitar and learn a new song.

I explored the nearest trusty Wal-Mart. I discovered there were zero Wal-Marts nearby which remained open for 24-hours. They all closed at midnight or 1:00 a.m. With those options, I chose a location I had observed other campers at. I made sure I had everything I needed so that once the Wal-Mart was closed, I was okay. The major item was a Gatorade bottle with a large opening. I had to use the Gatorade bottle in the back seat twice. The objective was to not look like I was peeing. Additionally, it was more important not to miss the bottle. I didn't want any urine on the sheets.

I pulled the sleeping bag over my body. My eyes closed as my mind wandered. I voiced in a whisper: *"You only fail when you stop trying. We have only one precious life, so do something extraordinary today even if it's tiny. A pebble starts the avalanche,"–K.A. Laity.*

Life was meant to be a magical journey and adventure. I truly believed I had much to be grateful for. I sensed the angels helping me. I gave daily thanks for the protective cloak surrounding me. I opened my heart to the universe and asked God to give me inspiration. I could conquer the world. I sensed each day I was closer to my dream. I had faith God was always nearby. I was jumping into a strong river current which was carrying me to places I had only imagined in my dreams.

Trust great things will happen. I maintained the belief that everything was already within me. I understood life may be filled with curves. It might change in the blink of an eye - one more reason to cherish each moment and move outside the norm. *We all die one day. Do not be afraid of death. By understanding death, we are empowered.* This reminded me how precious life was, how important it was to take a chance. *I might die tonight, the next day, or in 45-years.* I did not know when. So, I dreamt big, maintained unwavering faith, and seized the day.

The Tejano Monument
Austin, Texas State Capitol

CHAPTER 13
MARCH 23, 2016

Last night, the temperature was warmer than I had expected. I had purchased a small battery-operated fan. I had to use it to remain cool in the backseat. I slept without the sleeping bag to stay comfortable. I did not crack the windows for safety reasons. The wind was swirling in powerful gusts. It rocked the truck like a mother with a baby. I awoke three or four times during the night.

I had calculated to remain on budget of $2,000, I was allowed to spend about $20 per day. The goal was to generate the money by busking along with EP sales/donations. Yet, I had determined I was not going to be able to busk as much as I originally thought. What with the combination of driving, sight-seeing, locating a street or venue, perhaps both, plus the desire to compose and practice guitar…there were not enough hours in the day.

Likewise, I needed to add some break days to the schedule to relax and have opportunities to read, listen, and complete social media requirements.

When I awoke, I was determined to locate a spot to busk in Austin. I drove around downtown for almost two hours investigating hot sites where I thought street performers would set-up. I assumed they would be everywhere. I had driven around Austin for over four hours during my visit so far, and I had not yet seen one street performer. I saw an excellent wall mural on a building, which could act as a backdrop. It was on a red brick wall of a bar on the corner of a busy street. Unfortunately, there was no parking near the location and heavy construction was taking place nearby. I stopped at a paid lot around the corner, approximately two blocks away, but it cost $8 per hour to park. I thought it was a little steep. Instead, I left. Besides, the location would have been a bust: no one could hear me considering the commotion.

Overall, the downtown Austin area was quite boisterous. The combination of traffic and ongoing construction assaulted my ears. I continued driving in circles until the perfect spot opened. It was on Congress Street, near 6th street. There was an open parking spot near the Bank of America. I exited the truck with excitement and purchased a ticket for parking. The meter rate was only $1.50 for two hours. After paying for the parking, I approached the truck bed to unlock the black waterproof cover. I reached into a pocket, only to find it empty.

MARCH 23, 2016

The hardtop keys were missing. I searched everywhere in the truck, through clothes and bedding. Perhaps they had fallen from my pockets at some point. After about 10 minutes, I decided I had lost the keys. I contacted the key company. They told me for about $30 they could overnight a new set of keys to a local Fed-ex office. The customer rep stated I could use a screwdriver and break the lock. However, the remainder of the trip the belongings would be susceptible to thieves. I sat there stressed and thought about where the keys could have possibly fallen from my pocket. As the stress increased, my body temperature did too. I started to sweat. I concluded the keys could have either fallen from my pocket at the paid lot or earlier in the morning at the Wal-Mart. I exited the perfect parking space and drove back to the paid lot. I walked over to the meter, and thankfully there the keys were on the ground. I was so grateful and thanked God for the miracle. Not only did it save me from spending more money on keys along with the hassle of locating a Fed-Ex, it prevented me from staying another night in Austin. It also kept me from breaking the lock of the bed cover.

 I had the keys. With a thankful grin on my face, I decided it was time to locate a new parking spot. While in the parking lot, I realized I needed to use the bathroom. I spotted a nearby alley with trash cans. I walked over and began to use the bathroom behind a dumpster. Despite the strong urge to continue, I had to stop mid-stream because a construction guy thought I was inspecting his truck and tools. The mid-stream stoppage burned. I contemplated completing the original task, yet I noticed him walking towards me. I zipped my pants and walked back towards the truck. He stared at me; I was surprised he did not say anything or approach me.

I revisited the earlier location which I had paid for. Sadly, it was taken. Amazingly, though, they were preparing to back out. Thus, I experienced an additional moment of gratitude as I parked in the exact same spot again. I unloaded the musical equipment from the truck and set up away from the Bank of America entrance door. The intention was not to be a hindrance to the people walking along the street. The set up was a battery street amp with two pedals. I had a looper pedal and a booster pedal, a microphone stand, my "Elvis" microphone, and an iPad attached for lyrics. I started to play. Shortly into the first song, people noticed me and smiled. A security guard from the Bank of America building exited. He approached me with a thumb up. I was thankful. He could have easily told me to leave. As a matter of fact, he gave me a tip.

I street performed for 45 minutes with the amp and microphone. Out of the blue, I was approached by two bicycle cops. The policemen were cordial as I introduced myself. They told me Austin does not allow amplification without a permit. The cost was $150 at City Hall. The major issue of the permit was location specific. At purchase, a determined location was placed onto the permit - magnificent if I were a resident. I could lock down a location at which only I could street perform, perhaps become a local legend. Since I was passing through town briefly, it was a waste of time and money. I explained to the cops the purpose of the "Confessions of a Dreamer Tour." They agreed there was no reason to acquire a permit. They advised me I could continue, but to perform acoustically. The two cops departed on their bicycles. The Bank of America security guard returned and inquired what the cops had said. I explained to him I was only allowed to play without using the amp. If I continued, and they returned, I would be given a citation. He swayed with laughter. He removed his cell phone from his pocket and captured a picture along with my information. He purchased an autographed copy of my EP, *Crossroads*, and wished me well.

I played another hour in acoustic fashion. Unfortunately, with the combination of downtown traffic noise as well as construction racket, the acoustic guitar and my voice were hidden. Prior to the arrival of the police, a small gathering of people had encircled me, listening, providing tips with applause. After the police departed, people only walked past smiling. Some donated change or bills into the silver can. The highlight of busking was a couple visiting from Dallas who stopped to listen. We shared a brief conversation about music and the tour. He purchased an autographed EP and invited me to Dallas to perform at a keen venue there, if I were in town on Thursday. He hosted a songwriter's night and asked me to perform at it.

I cleared away the equipment and secured it under the lockable bed cover. I settled into the driver's seat, pondering. a*ll in all, I disposed of my comfort zone. I believed anything was possible. I had piloted my normal shy self to perform on a bustling downtown street in front of complete strangers. Thus, I uncovered an inner courage. Numerous people smiled, several people blessed the tip jar with money, and a few even snapped pictures and recorded video. It would had been wondrous to remained amped up. I cherished the way my voice and guitar sounded through the street amp of mine.*

It was about 4:00 p.m. Besides having the desire to write, I was wondering about what to do with the remainder of the day. There was a 24-Hour Fitness about 15 miles out of town. Considering I could not use my amp, I decided not to busk anymore. I did not desire any hassles or possible citations from the police.

Rather than driving to the gym, I returned to the Starbucks from the previous night. Unfortunately, it was crowded. There were no available outlets to plug my devices to charge and use. Though it was mobbed, at least I could use the restroom. I gazed into the mirror at a scruffy face. I would relish a long hot shower. Most of the other surrounding Starbucks which popped up on the internet closed around 8:00 p.m. or were inside a grocery store.

MARCH 23, 2016

I exited the Starbucks. I located a park to plan the rest of the day's adventure. The late-afternoon weather was pleasant, in the low 80s with a breeze. I selected an area in the shade. The breeze was refreshing. I savored the chosen space. Surveying the surroundings, I scribbled in my journal. An hour elapsed quickly. I had only purchased an hour of parking in their lot. I contemplated remaining as I noticed the red flag displaying on the parking meter next to the silver horse I rode. I departed, I was not willing to take the risk of having the truck towed or getting a ticket.

I noticed all the batteries for both iPads and the laptop were drained. The truck required gas as well. I would have to idle the engine to fully charge the devices. Before departing the park, I opened the bed cover for a quick snack. I realized the warmth and sunshine radiating over the black bed cover made the ice melt quickly in the cheap Wal-Mart cooler. I definitely needed to budget for a better cooler for future adventures, perhaps a Yeti.

I decided not to park somewhere to allow the truck to idle an hour or two to charge the devices. I yearned for a location to change clothes, which would also help me feel refreshed. I was becoming self-conscious and worried whether I had any body odor. I had not taken a shower for a couple of days. Though I had not perspired, I had done a three-hour bike ride the day before around the city of Austin and had slept inside the confines of the truck. I was bathing with those hunting wipes every night and each morning. Besides, I was trying my best to wear clean clothes each day. Nonetheless, I was close to needing a laundromat.

I thought about leaving Austin to locate a Starbucks which closed later than 8:00 p.m. It was distressing though. I was in the live music capitol of the world, and there I was, thinking about leaving. I was a songwriter. Would you not assume I desired to listen to live music, network, or say, "Tommy, you are single, at least adventure out to the bar for a drink and talk to a gorgeous Texas girl." Yet, I chose a different path.

My spirit was low. It was as if I were in a daze. It was quite an emotional transformation from earlier in the day. Earlier, performing, I was confident, excited, and alive. Currently, I desired to be alone surrounded by quiet. I believed in my abilities. I took risks. Were we not supposed to? Was it not the path to our dreams? I asked God to teach me, bless me with wisdom, understanding, and knowledge. I believed my intuition was the immersion of my soul into the currents of life. I affirmed that no matter how many detours or road blocks I encountered, I would continue moving forward toward my dreams.

50-Foot Waterfall
Hamilton Pool Preserve

CHAPTER 14

MARCH 24, 2016

A severe thunderstorm tore through Austin during the night. It rained and thundered while bolts of lightning danced across the sky. Due to the weather, I was not able to maintain a comfortable position in the truck. The booming thunder startled me each time. The pounding rain created a deafening ambience inside the cab. I did not sleep much, to say the least.

When I awoke in the morning, I had a sore neck. I had encountered a draft in the truck. The thunderstorm reduced the outside temperature by about 20 degrees.

I was contemplating traveling to the venue in Dallas where I'd been invited to perform by the couple who spoke to me on the street while I was busking. However, there were a few locations I preferred to investigate before heading toward Dallas.

Besides presenting my music, a separate goal of the "Confessions of a Dreamer Tour" was to stick to the backroads to see America, and to stop at rare locations to visit, preferably awe-inspiring free ones. Before departing Mississippi, I had researched unique, free locations recommended by different travel websites. I printed off a few lists and planned to check off as many as I could view.

I departed Austin and drove west on US-290. Approximately thirty minutes west of Austin, I reached Dripping Springs, Texas. It was home of the Hamilton Pool Preserve, a nature preserve that had been around for hundreds of years. It had two separate trails: a one-mile hike along a stream where it emptied into a vast body of water, and a shorter hike of about 0.2 miles to a pool of water fed by a 50-foot waterfall.

I chose to trek the stream route, initially thinking most people traveled to the waterfall. The stream's path was serene and quiet. Most of the trail was single track. The pathway itself was unique, as one walked through boulders and around strange trees and shrub formations. I crossed paths with another person along the way; one of us had to pause and step aside as the other passed. The stream ebbing next to the trail was remarkably clear with miniature waterfalls. I saw fish swimming along. The area was superbly protected. Neither the rock formations nor the trees had evolved much since the 1800s.

The trail ended at the river. The current moved swiftly. I could not see around either bend. There were some rock formations in the middle of the river but were located too far from shore to attempt to swim to. The sand was brownish in color and the water was in the high 50s, so this country boy who loves his water temperature in the mid-90s did not place a single toe into it! I did see a few swimmers. I had brought a GoPro camera, but when I attempted to use it, the battery was dead. It was frustrating, because I had checked the battery a few days before, and it was full. I had not turned it on or used it at all since then. It was the second time I had wanted to use the GoPro where the battery was dead. I guessed it did not hold its charge very long. On the return to the trailhead to connect to the waterfall trail, I paused to observe a few tiny trout swimming in the clear water. They slowly made their way against the current.

    I made my way to the pool of water where the waterfall first became visible. There was always something about waterfalls which I had loved. When I lived in Colorado in early 2000, there was a waterfall I could hike to, and I often did. Perhaps it's the power it produces, or simply the height, that created such a magical experience.

    The water at Hamilton Pool was surprisingly clear. The preserve had created a small beach where one could lay out and relax. It was constructed of whitish sand with pebbles. There was a walkway designed behind the waterfall, connecting to the beach. I relaxed on the beach for about an hour. I tested the water temperature by entering the chilly water up to my knees. It lasted less than two minutes. Many visitors were swimming as if they were in the hot waters of the Gulf of Mexico in the summertime. The warmth of the sun provided a delightful atmosphere. There were sprays of water from the surrounding rocks above, like a misting fan. The mist generated a cooling effect over my body. There were about 50 people on the beach. They were having a ball with family and friends, cherishing their moments together.

I withdrew from the waterfall to return to the parked truck. There was a picnic table where I was parked. I used the moment to enjoy a sandwich, chips, and fruit. Surrounding the area were trees and the sounds of nature.

I then embarked on a drive of about 20 minutes to reach Jacob's Well in Wimberley, Texas. Jacob's Well was an artesian spring. It allowed swimming, along with a cave which deep divers used. The water maintained a constant temperature of 68 degrees Fahrenheit. The cave, or Well, was 140 feet deep and almost a mile in length. The most fabulous aspect about it was, it was free to visit.

After I parked, I began the trek along the path to the Well. I arrived after walking about 20 minutes. I saw a group of young people swimming at the Well with their dog. Per the posted signs, swimming was not permitted until the end of May of 2016, and there were no pets allowed. From the various viewpoints I had, it did not suggest it was an interesting location to visit. It was a basic creek with the Well. The limestone cliffs I walked along overlooking the water were interesting. Except for the commotion of the group below, it was serene. I retreated to the attached nature center. The center had display boards describing the vegetation and possible wildlife in the area. Those boards demonstrated why the place was so popular. Inside the well at a depth of 140 feet or so, it opened to caves for exploration. I could not see the Well's opening from the cliff which I was standing on. According to the display boards, when the site was open for swimming, people jumped off the limestone cliff into the Well.

After the two scenic stops, I noticed it was already 2:30 p.m., so I began the drive to Dallas. I contemplated a hotel in Dripping Springs. Instead, I thought, perhaps I would splurge on a hotel in Dallas since it was Friday night. I could seek out some live music.

En route to Dallas on HWY-290 W, I reached a town named Johnson City. I stopped at the Roadrunner RV park to inquire the charge for a shower. The woman said, "$8." I thought it was too expensive just for a shower. I wished it were free. Before pulling away, I noticed a young man carrying three instruments. He had two facial piercings and a few more in each ear. He was walking across the street to busk at a restaurant. He told me he could profit $40 in an evening. He performed acoustically with no amplification. He alluded to another location near an old jail house. He busked there a few nights a week. It was a smaller restaurant. He provided directions to the location. The young man said the owner of the restaurant should be okay with me busking for a few hours outside. I drove away, leaving the city. About 15 minutes later, I began to think I should have taken him up on the other location. *I* was seeking to change myself with no regrets. Sadly, there was the regret of not at least trying, especially since busking and sharing music was the key theme to the Confessions of a Dreamer tour.

I soon reached a city called Marble Falls. It was 30 minutes north of Johnson City on US-281 N. I decided to stop at a Starbucks to catch up on social media and writing. There was a Wal-Mart Supercenter nearby where I could crash for the night. I researched locations to busk safely and legally in Dallas, as well as venues where I might be able to perform. Unfortunately, it being the weekend, most likely I could only listen to live music instead of performing. The perfect scenario would be to find a hotel near the venues of choice so I could walk to them.

I had slept five straight nights in the truck and had not taken a shower in three days. I was looking forward to stretching out to sleep and welcoming hot water against my skin in a shower. I was using bath wipe pads which helped keep my skin clean, and dry shampoo, but I would have liked to enjoy the comfort of a long hot shower.

I was driving in a part of Texas called the Hill Country. It was a geographical region located in the Edwards Plateau. The scenery was the heart and soul of Texas. There was a lot more elevation than I would have thought to find in East Texas. There were also a ton of breweries and wineries as I drove Highway 281 North.

I felt like I had failed the day. I had chosen not to street perform even when given a possible opportunity. Was it fear, or laziness? The sensation of guilt overflowed my being. To overcome the feeling, I devoured a Reese's peanut butter cup. I thought, when I became famous, I would have a rider for the dressing room. Besides stuff for my voice like water, tea, a humidifier, and throat spray, I would request Cheerwine and Reese's peanut butter cups.

After the peanut butter cup, I meditated. *Live life, Tommy. Do not worry about the how. Ask for it, believe it, feel it and have faith it will happen.* I trusted nothing was impossible. I believed a wonderful new world would open to Tommy Ray Music. I would continue to be kind, patient, and gentle with compassion. Understanding gratitude was the gateway to creating peace and happiness in my life. *Rise each day committed to taking an actionable step toward desires and dreams. Never say never. Visualize the dreams I desired. Believe in the possibilities.*

US Highway 281 North
The Hill Country of Texas
Marble Falls – Dallas, Texas

CHAPTER 15
MARCH 25, 2016

I had reached the current junction in my life because I persevered, confessing I deserved to add something, add value to the world. I was something bigger and better than I was just yesterday. I remained positive good times were ahead.

I drove nearly 200 miles. The first 100 miles on US-281 N, I noticed a simple fact: there was not a single fast food restaurant. The only restaurants I saw were BBQ and Mexican joints, mostly mom and pop versions. Once I reached Granbury, all changed. Granbury, Texas was roughly 70 miles outside of Dallas. I observed a square known as the Historic Granbury Square. It was lined with boutiques, home décor shops and eateries. The city boasted theatre and music, with a thriving art scene. I knew it would be an excellent location to spread Tommy Ray Music. Regrettably, I allowed my mind with its inner conversation of self-doubt to shut me down. Reluctance entered my world. I thought about transforming the tour into a visual tour only and utilizing open mic venues as the source of performances. I could simply stop at interesting locations and engage in activities along the way like hiking and mountain biking. I was holding onto the belief once I arrived in Oceanside, California, attitudes would change.

The tour up to this point had brought opportunities to achieve my goals. Perhaps I was naïve. When I was contemplating the "Confessions of a Dreamer Tour," the original dream had been to busk and perform at open mic venues. It had the added benefit of seeing America. It allowed for inspiration to compose new lyrics. Building confidence by listening to my heart was the correct pathway to live a life. I assumed I could merely park the truck, perform on any street corner with the amp, and earn tips and sell CDs. It had not been the reality. I was learning quickly busking was regarded as panhandling/begging. I simply desired to perform music as well as share the adventure. I preferred to use the small street amp and microphone instead of screaming over traffic.

I was confused by the different laws and contradictions. I was quite surprised: some internet posts stated busking was legal and easy, while others talked about being hassled by the police. Both of those comments were from the same cities (Austin, Dallas, etc.). The amplification laws were contradictory. One law explained one could not use an amp, another specified it was okay, but not after 10:30 p.m. A law said one could not utilize an amp to obtain people's attention, but the next law expressed one could use an amp if it could not be heard from 30 feet away. In the Dallas-Fort Worth area, one could not sell an album or CD while performing, without a special permit.

Though my spirit was low, in Granbury it was uplifted as I located a gym where I could exercise and take an extended hot shower. It would be my first shower in three days. After completing a two-hour work-out and delighting in a hot shower, I returned to the truck. I placed my head onto the seat rest, opened the visor mirror and stared into blue eyes. *There were gifts along my path. I was fulfilling my destiny.*

> "When you want something with all your heart, that is when you are closest to the Soul of the World. It is always a positive force."
> –Paulo Coelho.

> *I would focus on the present. Per Aristotle, "Knowing yourself is the beginning of all wisdom."*

> *Ralph Waldo Emerson wrote, "To be yourself in a world which is constantly trying to make you something else is the greatest accomplishment."*

I smiled to myself, closed the visor, and placed the truck into drive. I chose to have Fort Worth, Texas as my next destination.

The Supply House
Country Store

CHAPTER 16
MARCH 26, 2016

I was positioned at a picnic area on State Highway 114 West. A two-lane black top in Texas, the highway ran from Dallas-Fort Worth across Texas to the state border with New Mexico. I prepared some lunch and enjoyed the sun on my skin. The day was pleasant, with blue skies and a modest breeze. I heard cows in the distance. Luckily, their aroma was not noticeable. With each bite of the turkey and cheese sandwich, I considered how grateful I was for the opportunity. Under a Texas blue sky, there I was, following a dream and trusting an instinct. I was at this moment in time financially free and location independent.

When I awoke earlier in Granbury, I drove to Fort Worth, Texas. The thought of busking and performing on a street was my priority. I arrived after driving for 82 miles. I toured Fort Worth for about an hour, going into different areas. I never saw another street performer. I did not even see a police officer on a bike, which had become a common occurrence in those major cities.

I visited Sundance Square. Sundance Square was 35 blocks filled with dozens of options for shopping, dining, and entertainment. The square contained red-bricked streets, charming courtyards with lush landscaping. Without a doubt, was the location to street perform. However, it was quiet. It struck me as odd since it was a Saturday afternoon. There was hardly anyone walking around. I thought there would be lots of people shopping, sightseeing the numerous monuments, or eating at an outdoor café. I headed over to the Cultural District. The Cultural District offered six world class museums in a charming, park-like setting. The streets were empty. I occasionally saw a person or two walking by or admiring an outside exhibit, but it was nothing compared to Austin where the streets downtown was crowded with people all day, every day.

I continued touring around the Fort Worth area. Overall, it seemed a very pleasant city. It appeared clean and did not feel overcrowded. It offered the culture I craved, with lots of locations to walk and ride a bike. Fort Worth was another Texas city offering bike lanes through the downtown area, which was an excellent advantage.

I attempted to find a police station. I wanted to ask about the local regulations governing street performances. The internet posts I had skimmed through contradicted each other. Instead, I continued driving. I finally parked for a little break at a museum in the Cultural District. It was free parking, so I thought about going for a bike ride around the city. Once parked, I felt tired. Perhaps it was time to obtain a hotel room for the night and stretch out in a bed. I could use the time to wash my dirty clothes and complete the numerous desired tasks I strived for each day: practice guitar, compose lyrics, read, listen to motivational YouTube, etc...

Parked in the free lot with the windows cracked, a fresh spring breeze circulating, I decided not to explore the city. I decided to go toward the next major destination, Lubbock, Texas. I was in no hurry to arrive in Lubbock. Maintaining the backroads plan, the destination was five hours away. I would be arriving near sundown, if not later.

I encountered a downward moment in mood. I had driven 438 miles. I had street performed twice. I had performed twice inside a venue. A major failure of the original plan. My inner voice of self-doubt was intensifying. I had the courage to continue. Except, the excitement I normally sensed about my adventures was absent. I had exited my comfort zone and demonstrated dedication. Yet, was I mediocre? I desired to create a miracle. Was fear overtaking me?

As I pushed on toward Lubbock on TX-114-W, I paused at a picnic area along the highway, after about an hour of driving. At the picnic area, I opened the tailgate and sat shirtless underneath the sun. The sun caressed my skin warmly. I had become quite pale since I left Florida in 2012; I was not out in the sun much anymore. I carefully monitored my exposure to avoid any burns. I closed my eyes to allow my sense of hearing to lead. The sound of birds resonated through the nearby trees as leaves swayed from the power of the breeze. The aroma of a fresh cut field filled the air. As I said thank you and demonstrated my gratitude, I opened my eyes. I focused my attention on lunch.

After the lunch of a can of SpaghettiOs with meatballs, I was cleaning a pan I had used when a Suburban pulled up. A man exited the truck and asked if I were camping. I politely stated no, and I explained the tour. I was a little leery at first, as I was there alone. I had two handguns for personal protection. I had a mind set to fear or have suspicion of strangers. He told me he lived in Fort Worth and was returning from dropping off his daughter. He invited me to join him in a 420 break. Since I never partake when I might be drug-tested, I declined. Though my dream was to travel, write, and play music, which meant enjoying a high would not cause any future harm, the little voice was there in the back of my head. It said, *"There is a chance after the trip I may have to return to work as a physician assistant. If drug tested, I may fail."* Afterwards, I recalled a Will Smith video. Only have a plan A. If one had a plan B, such as my returning to medicine, most likely, it was one's final destination. Besides, I thought, what if whatever he offered me were laced with something? As he took tokes, we discussed medicine and how the tour was progressing. He shared how he was well provided for at work: great salary and reasonable hours. Nonetheless, he had encountered stagnation analogous to what 90 percent of Americans probably had. He mentioned he would love to be able to possess some freedom to follow his dreams. I extended to him an autographed EP. I asked if he would share it with his social circles. Before he pulled away, he donated $20 for the EP. *I was truly blessed. I was sitting at a picnic area in the middle of a two-lane black top deep in the back country of Texas. I sold an EP and inspired someone with my journey. I was truly grateful. Anything was possible.*

I noticed a plaque about 50 yards away on the side of the roadway. It displayed a historical fact about the area. I recalled seeing those plaques often during the drive. At each plaque was a pull-off to allow people to read the plaque safely.

I thought a positive benefit of traveling those backroads were the ability to observe the history of our country first hand, to observe things I never knew existed. I imagined settlers on their wagons gazing upon the same land I was looking at. I later enjoyed stopping from time to time to read those plaques about a battle, or how a distinct area was once a settlement.

A negative of traveling those backroads, depending on one's own personal views, was my phone had no service. It was a positive for me, personally, having no distractions. It allowed me the opportunity to listen to motivational speakers on the radio, through CD's, to pray, and simply to talk to myself in a positive, caring, and loving matter.

I had a vision once I arrived in California, the busking lifestyle would be looked upon in a different light than it had been perceived in the places I had seen so far. Since the start of the tour, busking had had dirty vibes. The two experiences were positive. Yet, when speaking to others about street performing, it seemed it was looked upon similarly to panhandling. Busking should be considered beautiful: art, and a way of expression. Many articles I had read claimed busking added an important element of culture to the cities. It was certainly what I believed. However, it appeared some cities deliberately created a difficult atmosphere to busk.

As I was driving away from the most recent stop, my original thought was to drive about another hour and find a hotel room. But as I came to each town along the highway, I discovered they were quite small with not much to offer, only tiny roadside motels. I decided to keep driving, thinking the next town would offer what I desired. With the thought in mind, before I knew it, I ended up in Lubbock.

As I was driving through those backroads of Texas, I decided not to listen to the radio for general music. I focused on inner thoughts as my eyes took in the beautiful surroundings. I had faith I would hear God through my instincts and know where the journey was supposed to go next. The thought of busking less and performing at more open mics crept into my mind. Most cities had open mics on Mondays through Thursdays. I could perform during those, then I could sightsee Friday through Sunday or observe different live performances and network. I began to wonder if I was the wrong man for the job of "Busking Across America" (which was the original title of the book).

When I arrived in Lubbock, I read it was considered the center of the South Plains in northwest Texas. The city was formed in 1890. It was home of Buddy Holly.

A major observation I made was how different it was from the other Texas cities I had visited. It resembled Jackson, Mississippi. It only contained a few tall buildings and had a quiet downtown area. As I approached Lubbock on the two-lane country black top road, there were no signs stating I was entering a city. Upon arrival, I drove through the downtown area. It was completely silent. I saw nothing open, no people walking around, or any cars parked along the street. It was not until I came upon Texas Tech when I saw a strip of bars, restaurants, and stores.

I chose to eat near the University at a sports bar. I decided to get a hotel room for the night. I wanted to stretch out in a bed, enjoy a hot shower, and wash clothes. I searched Hotels.com and located a hotel with good customer reviews under $100. It was only 10 minutes away from the University. As I listened to the GPS, it guided me away from the University, and the city unfolded into a much larger area. It contained a complex Interstate system, shopping malls, restaurants, and large office buildings.

After I checked into the room, I thought about the day's trip. The drive was along two-lane black tops with nothing on either side but ranch after ranch. Some of those ranches stretched at least 20 miles along the highway, so there was no telling how large they really were. I had seen cows, bulls, goats, and horses grazing on the grass at each ranch. The terrain had varied from flat to rolling hills, and then back to flat again. As I had scanned the terrain, I had visualized what it must have been like to ride through the area on horseback a hundred years before, or to run from the law trying to hide out in the harsh terrain back in the days of the Wild Wild West.

I began reading *The Prayer of Jabez* by Bruce Wilkinson. On page 47, the subject matter pertaining to my current mood was mentioned. *Per Dr. Mitchell, the feeling of 'I just cannot do it,' was what I was supposed to be feeling. It was expected when one attempted to do something large enough where failure was guaranteed unless God stepped in. When one dreams big and then decides to go for it, it goes against common sense. It contradicts our previous life experience. It sets us up to look like fools and losers if we fail. Dependence upon God makes heroes of ordinary people. I was reminded of recording my EP,* Crossroads. *I had traveled three times to Hit Music Studios in Spencer, North Carolina. I had remained in the studio for four days recording voice layovers to the music created by producer*

Jimm Mosher. The finalized project was created. It had sold less than 300 copies at $5 per EP, even though I had over 800 Facebook friends and family. I was becoming more emotional with each new day. Whenever I read inspirational passages, quotes or heard some beautiful music, I was moved to tears.

I listened to Ambrose Redmoon, "Courage is not the absence of fear, but rather the judgment that something else is more important than fear." To obtains what I desired, I needed to show up. Which was required to remain present. I had to remove myself from my comfort zone. Courage was taking tiny, tiny steps in the correct direction even though sometimes it was terrifying to do. By taking one step at a time in the right direction, it took active choices to create the life I dreamed of. I must continue to find the courage to pursue what I truly desired, to focus on what I could do right then to go in the direction of my goals. I had to trust the path would unfold, and to maintain the unwavering faith. I wanted to look back on my life and know I did everything I could to create the life I desired.

Prairie Dog Town
Mackenzie Park
Lubbock, Texas

CHAPTER 17

MARCH 27, 2016

I thought about remaining in Lubbock through Monday night, a three-night stay. I located a venue I could perform at Monday night. There was a website listing open mics all over the country. The venue in Lubbock was The Bluelight Live. Monday nights was their Songwriter night.

The Bluelight Live appeared to be a marvelous local bar with the best open mic situation. They embraced the art of songwriting and the ability to share original work with a room of listeners.

After waking up on Sunday morning, I was refreshed. I had probably slept almost 12 hours. I indeed relished the long steaming shower. Instead of the breakfast I usually prepared, I chose to eat in their restaurant. I devoured two plates of scrambled eggs, sausage, pancakes, and some fruit. After breakfast I packed my belongings, and then I checked out. I thought I could spend the next two nights in the truck. Though I had to admit, it had been rejuvenating to stretch out in a bed. I imagined a lazy day of naps and completing a few tasks if I were in the room until Tuesday morning.

I vacated the hotel. The weather presented a blue-sky day with a refreshing breeze. It was splendid. The temperature was in the high 50s, maybe low 60s. It was a shock since the day before it had been almost 80 degrees in Fort Worth.

I decided to drive to McKenzie Park. It contained the Joyland Amusement Park, Prairie Dog Town, a disc golf and regular golf course. The Brazos River flowed through. I located a quiet location with a picnic table near the Yellow House Draw stream. Considering it was Sunday, the park was jam-packed with families. Each gathering had their grill, music, and activities. The food's aroma danced through the air. The bouquet of grilled chicken, steaks, hamburgers, and hot dogs was wondrous. I saw an old car show in one section. I considered checking it out.

I perched on the picnic table's bench seat located underneath a tree. I gathered the books which I studied out of every day and began to read. *I believed the words and ideas written in The Alchemist* and *Warrior of the Light,* both by Paulo Coelho. They encouraged one to persevere to the end of the journey. I understood those books are not the Bible; however, they spoke to me deeply.

I sat there thinking about how I was encouraging others. *I had learned people would like to chase their dreams, but lacked the courage. Perhaps with the "Confessions of a Dreamer Tour," along with the book, I could inspire them to dream big and take a chance. I had touched at least four lives on my travels to date. I was grateful and blessed. I had unwavering faith I could inspire many more.*

I completed the reading task and contemplated a quick nap. The combination of the shade and the breeze created a peaceful ambience. Instead, I decided to fight the urge. If I stayed awake, perhaps I could sleep longer at night without waking up.

A positive aspect of the location was I had phone service. I searched Google to locate a gym. I thought I could work out later in the day and take a hot shower if they offered one.

Before arriving at McKenzie Park, I read they had a prairie dog park inside. It was free and open from dawn to dusk. The Prairie Dog Town had been around since the 1930s. I viewed hundreds of prairie dogs playing in their habitat. I got a package of baby carrots from the cooler to feed them. They chased them down and sat up on their hind legs and chomped away. It was very entertaining.

I remained at the park for a few hours. I peered at prairie dogs, read, wrote in my journal, and practiced guitar. Afterwards, I located a laundry to wash and dry my clothing. At the laundromat, I prepared some lunch while waiting on the dryer to finish. I folded everything and stowed them away in the plastic container. I cleaned the bed of the truck as well as the inside of the cab. I made a list of supplies which I needed. The only other chore or obligation for the day was to locate a grocery store and restock.

I was overjoyed I was on tour. Many times, along the way, I wished for companionship. To share the adventures, thoughts, and hear someone's laughter would be pleasant. It was one aspect which struck me when I watched the movie Into the Wild. *The main character performed all his adventures alone, like I was doing. I had completed almost all my personal adventures in my life alone. Yet, in the end, he wrote how life should be shared. Perhaps one day my adventures would be shared. It was once said in* Warrior of the Light, *"The closer you get to realizing the dream you set for yourself, the more difficult things become. In the pursuit of your dream, you are constantly subjected to tests to ensure you remain persistent to reveal your courage." Perhaps it was why not everyone reached their dreams and so many decided to stop dreaming. They stopped before their breakthrough. I believed the universe was making an effort to help me succeed as I pursued my dreams.*

CHAPTER 18

MARCH 28, 2016

I crashed in the truck last night. I followed the Wal-Mart parking lot routine. First, I selected a parking spot. I parked next to a shopping cart return stall, in the vicinity of a security light. I parked the passenger side of the truck to the return stall because it was where my head was. Then I walked inside. I strolled around the store for a bit. I then entered the restroom to brush and floss my teeth. I returned to the truck and climbed into the back seat. I placed shirts on hangers over the back glass and both back windows. I applied the black sleep mask, curled up like a little child and fell to sleep. Sometimes there was a WiFi signal where I was parked. I could watch a movie on my iPad or my cellphone. I tried not to enter the Wal-Mart until the next morning unless I had a restroom emergency.

In the morning, I re-entered the store to brush my teeth and wash my face. Based on how hungry I was, I either ate at the McDonalds or Subway inside, or prepared a cold breakfast from the truck (a spoon of peanut butter, cashews, almonds, and an apple). I returned to the truck and cleaned myself with the camping wash wipes and dressed in fresh clothes. It was the "Confessions of a Dreamer Tour" routine. Last night, at The Bluelight Live, was the songwriter's night. I had contacted the venue the day before. The open mic roughly began at 9:00 p.m. In Mississippi and most other open mics I had attended in the past, 7:00 p.m. was the start time. A 9:00 p.m. start time was late, especially for a Monday night, I thought. However, it was why I was out there. I did not have to arise early the next morning. I was on tour to share music. Except, it was only 7:30 a.m. I had a long day to occupy.

I located a Barnes and Noble. It was a great place to utilize free WiFi and finish my reading and my social media account obligations. A wonderful aspect about a Barnes and Noble was I could use it like a library. Whatever topic I was reading about or desired to research, I simply walked to the shelf, located the topic, read what I needed and placed the book back on the shelf.

I killed about three hours there. Seeing the time and realizing I may not be performing until after 9:00 p.m., I resolved the best course of action, besides eating lunch, was to return to a hotel. I could relax and have a location to continue completing needed tasks. An advantage as well was I would have a room to return to after the performance. I figured if I did not get a room in the early afternoon, I would end up driving around the city for seven hours wasting gas.

My mind drifted into thought. *I surrendered to the divine light. I allowed His gifts and powers to reveal themselves. I believed those gifts and powers would take care of my life and would influence my day-to-day existence. I believed in the silence of my heart, I would hear an order to guide me. I had to be patient and allow room for the Universe to act. I know my intuition was God's language.*

By continuing to listen to the wind and talking to the stars most people might say I was mad, illogical, or lived in a fantasy world. Though I trusted I was listening to my heart, I believed it knew all things. I had discovered things along the way I never would have seen had I not had the courage to try new things which seemed impossible to achieve. I do know the Universe tested everything I learned before my treasures were located. It was not meant to be evil, but to ensure I had courage and unwavering faith. Those tests helped me master the lessons required to learn.

CHAPTER 19

MARCH 29, 2016

I awoke still in Lubbock, Texas. I had been there since Saturday, for a total of three nights and four days. I was lying in bed, covered with blankets, in the hotel room. It was about 10:15 a.m. The reason I had remained was to perform the previous night at the singer-songwriter night at the Bluelight Live. I had every intention of performing.

After I checked into the same hotel from the other night around 4:00 p.m. I darkened the room and slipped into sleep. I slept about an hour or so.

As I watched the clock move forward, something happened to me. I lost all desire to perform or to share Tommy Ray Music. I wanted only to remain in bed. I wasted the entire evening watching movie after movie. I was a little lost. I think it was the first test and wall which I experienced along the tour. I wasn't at the point of giving up and going home. Nevertheless, I began to want to sightsee rather than street perform. I was angry with myself because of regret. The inner fear of rejection was building. I sensed shame. I turned my head away from the mirror, sensing the failure. My negative EGO was compounding the pessimistic inner talk. I remained in the queen size bed, curled into a fetal position, grasping at a pillow and blankets. I grabbed my iPad and tuned into YouTube. I spent the next hour listening to motivational videos from Les Brown, amongst others. It reduced the negative inner dialogue and returned my optimistic attitude.

People told me I had talent. They enjoyed my lyrics and songs. Yet when I performed live, I always perceived the applause was courtesy rather than enthusiasm. I would like to have believed people listened to me and thought, "Wow, you were awesome, and performing was what you should be doing full-time."

I sold more EPs when I simply explained my music and the "Confessions of a Dreamer Tour" compared to the nights I performed live. I loved to write and compose, whether it was songs, books, or in my journal. I wondered if the new songs I was composing were really songs or poems: perhaps a combination of both. I had the desire to choose a few of them and participate in an open poetry mic to see what people thought. I became more positive.

I considered the past few days as falling down. I had not failed. I understood I needed to simply brush off my knees and continue moving forward. I enjoyed performing on the street in Austin, so why was I avoiding

MARCH 29, 2016

performing? I had to close my eyes and ask. I prayed as I drove further west, and my attitude reversed to excitement. I delighted in performing. I was alive. Which was why the previous night had been difficult. I had an opportunity to perform at a major songwriter's night, yet, I chose not to take it.

I departed Lubbock around noon. The next destination would probably be Roswell, New Mexico. As I exited the hotel, a wind blowing 30 mph grabbed my attention. A circular force made it difficult to open the truck doors. I placed a few sheets of new lyrics I was writing on the passenger seat. They disappeared in an instant.

The wind escalated to about 40 mph for most of the trip. The drive to Roswell was about 174 miles. I chose US-380 W as the route. I paused at a rest area to prepare some lunch and to enjoy the scenery. I had to remain inside the truck to eat, as the wind was so strong. It literally swayed my body from side to side when I tried to eat at a picnic table.

I considered a side trip to some caverns. They were located almost two and a half hours south of where I was. Instead, I proceeded forward. I listened to motivational tapes as I drove and broke out into tears at times from the inspirational messages. *I believed I was conducting similar lessons which those individuals had adapted to obtain their goals. I trusted around the next curve or over the next hill, another breakthrough would materialize. I maintained unwavering faith someone had heard my music or discovered my writings. In doing so, it would help create the miracle I was in search of.*

I arrived in Roswell, New Mexico at 4:30 p.m. I was in the southeastern quarter of the state. The city was most popularly known for having its name attached to the Roswell UFO incident. It was a popular town for tourists around the country due to the many alien-themed stores, restaurants, museums, among other attractions. They even had a McDonald's built in the form of a flying saucer. The city of Roswell was established in 1873.

The drive to Roswell was mostly pancaked terrain offering visions of oil rigs and cattle. The robust winds of 40 mph made the truck weave on the highway from time to time as I proceeded on the journey. The weather was a favorable 80 degrees with dazzling blue skies. It was awe-inspiring, gazing at the distant horizon. The colors it created were fascinating. Besides the horizon, I gazed off to the left and to the right for what seemed over 100 miles. The expansive views made one almost think the world was flat. At a few points, it seemed over the next hill, the world would drop off to a body of water or a darkened abyss. The skyline on the right had a grayish hue, while on the left it remained blue.

When I arrived in Roswell, I was delighted. It offered everything I depended upon. It had a grocery store for restocking supplies, a Starbucks for a hot tea and free internet, along with a 24-hour Wal-Mart to serve as an overnight camping area.

MARCH 29, 2016

While inside the Starbucks, I researched the local music scene. Nothing popped up on the internet or in their local newspaper for an open mic night. Instead, I lounged there a couple of hours. I read and wrote in my journal and completed my social media obligations.

The skies transitioned to darkness with nightfall. I exited Starbucks to my final destination of the evening: Wal-Mart. I located a safe parking space with all the aspects I preferred. I crawled into the backseat cave. After a few moments of locating a comfortable position, I closed my eyes to another day along the "Confessions of a Dreamer Tour."

Alien Autopsy
Roswell, New Mexico

CHAPTER 20
MARCH 30, 2016

I was surprised I slept so well the first night in Roswell, in the truck. I remained asleep from 9:00 p.m. until almost 8:00 a.m. the next morning with limited waking up throughout the night. After awakening, I located a grocery store to restock basic food staples. I never chose to purchase food items from a Wal-Mart after reading quite a few articles stating how lousy most of the items I enjoyed were. I drove through the main street inspecting Roswell. I noticed a lot of sci-fi store fronts. I decided not to linger and proceeded on the tour. The day's goal was to head towards Albuquerque, New Mexico.

Albuquerque was a three-hour drive northwest. I took US-285 N. Though I had slept through the night with only a few bouts of wakefulness, I suffered fatigue for most of the trip. I almost stopped to take a nap. I continued fighting the sleepiness. The most difficult aspect of the trip was wanting to stop every 10 miles or so to snap landscape pictures. The manner in which the clouds drifted, powered by the wind, with the mountains in the distance, was stunning. I envisioned the skies illuminated at night with stars blanketing the heavens.

I arrived in Albuquerque, the most populous city of New Mexico. It hedges on the Rio Grande. In the distance, I could see the Sandia Mountains. Albuquerque was well known for the International Balloon Fiesta, the world's largest gathering of hot-air balloons from around the world.

A previous online search informed me in order to street perform in Albuquerque, a permit was required. On a positive note, the permit was free. I located City Hall with Google Maps on the cell phone. Unfortunately, the only two people who could sign the permit were not available when I arrived. The woman inside the office copied my information. She explained normally the permit was delivered by email. I explained I was only in town for one day. I asked them to call me if at all possible. She agreed, and I departed City Hall to explore the city.

During the tour around the city, I located the ABQ BioPark next to the Rio Grande. It offered mountain biking trails along the river. I planned to do some within the next day or two before leaving the city. I was indecisive about how long I would remain in Albuquerque. It depended on the permit and on finding locations to perform. I happened upon Old Town. It was a historic plaza founded in 1706. It had restaurants, hotels, bed & breakfasts, and museums. There were over 150 stores with quiet hidden courtyards and gardens to stroll through. Supposedly, the location was open for street performers, if they had the permit.

I spoke with a few shop owners, and they pointed to a spot where most people performed. It was a gazebo in front of the San Felipe de Neri Church. It was a popular location where people passed to take photographs. I chatted with a policeman. He stated I could perform inside the gazebo, but not ask for tips or sell my EPs. And I could perform around the square, just not on the main sidewalk. I would have to perform around the corners of the shops. I observed one person busking acoustically. Most of the people selling trinkets to the tourists sat on blankets on the main sidewalk with their backs against the storefront walls.

I continued walking and noticed a square off the main road which had a few shops and restaurants. I spoke with several business owners and learned the people who owned a Mexican restaurant also owned the entire square. In terms of the law, it was private. It was open to the public but not operated under city rules. They provided permission to perform the next day during lunch with my street amp. The news lifted my spirits. I had an opportunity to share music as well as to reap tips.

Afterward, I drove to the downtown area where all the bars were located. I would need a busking permit to perform on the streets there. I observed all the popular music venues. The area was part of historic Route 66. People told me at night it was illuminated in neon. They described the luminous bulbs of neon pinks, blues, and greens.

I was blessed to locate a gym in Albuquerque. Not only could I work out, the gym offered a shower as well. I had hoped all the 24-Hour Fitness gyms had showers. Sadly, only a handful had them so far on the journey.

I located a Starbucks after finishing up at the gym. The internet stated Nob Hill was a great place. It was considered a historic district. It was crowned, "Albuquerque's original Main Street." It was situated near the New Mexico University. It offered live music, art, dancing, film and theater, shopping, and dining. I planned to visit either tonight or the next day to scope it out.

I thought after I performed the next day, if I had not yet heard from City Hall, I would return and attempt again to obtain a permit. With a permit, I could utilize the street amp downtown at Nob Hill and perform.

I located numerous other gym locations, which meant I could work out without being restricted to a certain area in town. Most importantly, I could shower daily.

After looking around the other sections of the city, I returned to the normal routine: I searched for another Starbucks and a 24-hour Wal-Mart.

With my head upon the pillow, I contemplated. *It was worth it. Taking a leap of faith to dream big. I was investing in myself. I had the potential to create. It might be scary. There were over a million reasons to stop or to not try. However, one risk may create the dream world which I imagined. I understood there were no guarantees. Afterwards, people might say, "I told you so." No matter, it was the first step of a journey. I was stretching myself. I was alive. I believed it was worth it. I knew I could fall. It did not matter. Life was short.*

Old Town Albuquerque
Albuquerque, New Mexico

CHAPTER 21

MARCH 31, 2016

Last night, I had difficulty falling asleep. I tossed and turned in the backseat of the truck until midnight. I awoke at 2:00 a.m. and was unable to return to sleep until almost 3:30 a.m. I did not know if it was because the temperature dropped below 40 degrees or because the night before I was asleep by 8:30 p.m. and slept almost until 9:00 a.m. the next morning. I had been told numerous times Albuquerque was a dangerous city, but I was safe and secure in the parking lot of a 24-hour Wal-Mart. I did not sense it was security concerns that kept me from sleeping.

When I awakened, I was dismayed at the morning temperature of 34 degrees. I was performing outside at 11:30 a.m. I thought I could not do it unless I applied about three layers of clothing. I debated if people would be outside to shop at Old Town on a colder day. I considered backing out.

Once awake, I steered to the gym. My desire to exercise was low. Primarily, I wanted a hot shower. I briefly worked out. I completed the long hot shower but forgot to shave. After the shower, I placed two layers of clothes on. Blessfully, when I walked outside the gym around 11:00 a.m. I was surprised how quickly it had warmed. I recalled in the dryer areas of the country, the cold does not cut through you like on the East Coast. I left the gym and returned to the private square in Old Town. By the time I sat up the equipment in the square, I was wearing a short sleeve shirt, even though the temperatures never reached the 60s.

I performed outside, inside the square's boundaries, for about three hours. I had assumed there would be limited foot traffic on a Thursday afternoon, in a private square a few blocks away from the normal high-visited landmarks. Instead of being downcast, I used it as practice and performed every song I knew. I treated each song as if I was performing to a sold-out stadium. I gave it my all.

Overall, about 30 people walked by during the three-hour set. A few passersby nodded, others smiled, and a few took pictures or created a video. I was complimented on my voice a few times. I earned a few tips, $5 in total. Nonetheless, for me, it wasn't about the money. Once again, I had touched someone and made them smile. Besides, I had always been a quiet person. Yet, there I was in public singing, playing guitar in front of strangers. It was a confidence builder. I could accomplish anything and everything. Of course, I wished they would have all thrown in five or ten-dollar bills and purchased an EP!

When I finished performing, I had lunch at the Mexican restaurant. I wanted to thank them for allowing me to perform. Also, I could never turn down authentic Mexican food. At the table during lunch, I thought about the day's outing. I had performed all the songs of my 45-song repertoire. I made some mistakes; though the iPad for lyrics was in front of me, I forgot lyrics at times because I attempted to turn away and use my memory. I determined which ones I considered I was most comfortable with, along with the songs which highlighted my talent. I was a laid back, slower tempo artist. Performing on the streets, I was relaxed compared to on the stage. I believed I placed more heart and soul into the songs when I was more relaxed. I was capable of about three and a half hours of songs. Yet, I thought only one and a half hours of the songs were strong. I determined the tempo of those songs I preferred were too slow for a bar setting. I had learned bars were in search of high energy musicians performing the top hits from the radio which the patrons knew. Through research I found Nashville, Tennessee offered nightly songwriter showcases and the style I enjoyed performing was in demand. A person in the audience during the day had stated I would do well in Portland, Oregon. He said my voice and the way I came across as I sang would be a positive combination in Portland.

I was going to perform that night at a local coffee shop. Unfortunately, their webpage did not mention the open mic information like the local paper did. Besides, my voice was sore after three hours of singing. I chose not to visit the coffee shop.

When I finished the day, I returned to a Starbucks to complete a few assignments. I checked emails and discovered I had received one from a radio station in Houston, Texas. The gentleman complimented me on a cover of "Wagon Wheel" I had posted on YouTube. He asked me to contact him. I wrote a thankful email.

I trusted the moment was now. Jim Rohn stated, "On any day you can massively change the direction of your life." I was completing the baby steps each day to follow his advice. I wanted to accomplish many things in life. I was itching to take crazy risks. To be the best I could be. I continuously reminded myself to have a smile of gratitude on my face.

I stopped worrying about other people's opinions. I was following my heart to accomplish my dreams. I was creating a worthwhile future while enjoying each moment. I performed the needed tasks each day to move forward. I sensed with enough baby steps, the results would appear. With consistency, the goals would be obtained. A major goal of mine was to be on my death bed with a heart filled with gratitude. To

MARCH 31, 2016

know I had a crazy life filled with experiences, memories, and believing I brought inspiration and value to the world.

I continued the "Confessions of a Dreamer Tour" by putting one foot forward each day. I was creating changes in my life which brought me joy.

The Land of Fire and Ice
Ice Cave and Bandera Volcano
Grants, New Mexico

CHAPTER 22
APRIL 1, 2016

The original plans were to mountain bike along the Rio Grande River Trail first thing in the morning. When I awoke, it was only 37 degrees. The positive aspect about camping at a Wal-Mart was if I required anything like food, a restroom, or even truck supplies, it was all right there under one roof.

Before departing the Wal-Mart, I noticed I needed a new driver's side headlight. After I replaced it with a new lamp, I drove to the gym for a full workout. I maintained the thought it might be warm enough to ride my bike around 11:00 a.m. The day before, the weather had warmed significantly around the same time.

After a work-out and a lengthy hot shower, I walked outside the gym and began cleaning up the truck. I re-arranged items to make certain things more accessible. I checked the cooler to inspect the ice levels. Once again, the ice was melted. As I was performing those tasks, I saw a homeless man searching through the nearby garbage bin for items to use, perhaps even to eat. I walked over to him and asked if he were hungry. He said yes. I mentioned I could not give him money, but I could give some sandwich stuff. He smiled and thanked me. As we talked, he told me he had been homeless for about five years. He was part of a group of six other homeless people. They acted as a family. Each one went out each day finding as much as they could to bring back to the group so they could all share. I offered him the remaining turkey deli meat and cheese with a loaf of bread. I added two cans of pasta. As we talked further, I asked if he needed water. I gave him one of the gallon jugs when he said yes. I then thought the ice chest was too large for what I needed, and the ice melted within two days. So, I gave it to him as well. Finally, I asked him if he needed the most cherished item I owned, toilet paper. When he said yes, I offered him two rolls. In return, he provided a pamphlet about local free services around the Albuquerque area. I could use the information for medical services or a place to stay. In theory, I was homeless myself. I had some money saved up, but I was living out of the truck. He shook my hand and he departed with his loaded down shopping cart.

Though I myself was living on borrowed money, attempting to make money busking, it was difficult to observe someone in his situation. I was grateful I could help him in a small way. I would rather increase my credit card bill than pass on helping someone in need, especially knowing they were about to eat from a garbage can.

After the experience, the temperature was warm enough to go ride my bike. Besides, when would I ever be there again? So, I went to the Rio Grande Park. I put on my warm Nike gear, headband, and gloves. When I was removing the bike from the truck, I noticed a dent in the bike rack. Had I hit something or had someone hit me? I did not recall hitting anything. The location of the dent on the bike rack made me realize my bike could not have been on it at the time of impact. So, someone must have hit it during one of my previous rides.

I led off down the concrete path and headed towards the dirt trail. I planned to use my GoPro camera to capture the adventure. The first trail was a single lane track offering a few close views of the Rio Grande. The dirt was hard packed, creating an easier riding surface. I rode for about a mile; it was entertaining. In Mississippi, I normally rode along the asphalt bike path, never through nature on dirt. I was able to jump a few hills, but nothing major.

I approached a platform which allowed viewing of nature and picture taking. I closed my eyes. The trail made me aware of my seclusion. I could have been in the middle of nowhere. The wind carried the sounds of water and birds.

Everything was wonderful until I transitioned to the North trail. I stopped to drink some water and adjust the GoPro. A young homeless man approached me. He was a young guy in his 20s, had no bags or backpacks, or any other kind of possessions with him. He appeared out of nowhere. He attempted to talk to me and ask questions. However, I was not comfortable with the interaction. So, as politely as I could, I began to ride back towards the truck. I understood I was a guy, but I had my GoPro, my phone, and my bike. If he tried to take them, especially if he had a weapon, there was not much I could have done. Yet, I would have aimed to protect everything belonging to me.

When I returned to the truck, I immediately packed. I wanted to depart quickly in case the young man came up to the parking lot and saw me at the truck. As I was pulling out, I saw four or five young kids on bikes heading in the direction I had just come from. *I said a prayer they would be safe and have fun.*

I departed Albuquerque. I was at peace. I busked a few hours, exercised, showered, and helped another person. I was truly grateful. I was successful in Albuquerque, New Mexico.

I chose to split town via the Interstate 40-W. I proceeded for about an hour before locating US-60-W. It was a two-lane blacktop road towards Arizona. The landscapes along the route were majestic. One section contained plains overrun with ranches. Then the landscape suddenly transformed into cliffs emerging into large bluffs.

APRIL 1, 2016

The colors varied from greens, beiges, reds and black. The clouds hovering over the bluffs were astonishing. I wished I were a bird dancing among them.

As I traveled, I approached a sign for an upcoming roadside attraction, "The Land of Fire and Ice." My curiosity got the best of me, and I stopped. For $12, I could hike two separate short trails. One trail was to an ice cave, a collapsed lava tube. The longer one along a path of lava rocks until you reached the remnants of the Bandera Volcano. I chose to walk to the ice cave first. As I walked, something occurred which I had not witnessed since 2002. Flurries of snow began to drift down. As it continued, I began to worry the trip would be delayed by unexpected weather. I did not have snow tires or 4-wheel drive on the pick-up truck. I discovered it was fun walking through a snow flurry. It added a sense of adventure. The negative aspect was the GoPro camera was not working to reveal to everyone what I was experiencing. Instead, I used my cell phone to capture pictures and videos.

The ice cave was unique. I entered by walking down a few flights of wooden steps. The combination of the wood and snow created a slippery surface. I stood on a platform looking down into the cave. When I originally stopped at the attraction, I thought I would be walking through an ice cave like I did when I was a kid in Rock City, Tennessee. The cave remained 31 degrees no matter the temperature outside. The floor of the cave was a slab of ice at least 20 feet thick. The self-guided pamphlet stated the deepest ice dated back 3,400 years, which was probably why they didn't want anyone walking on it. The view inside was perpetual ice along with natural cave formations. The cave had an interesting green tint to it, as well, and because the cave was subtly lit with the outside ambience, no lighting implements were required.

I back-tracked on the trail towards the Bandera Volcano. It was called the Bandera Crater. It was 800 feet deep. It had erupted about 10,000 years ago. The lava flowed from the eruption nearly 23 miles. The trail itself began at the base of the volcano. When I reached the lookout point after a half mile walk, I was standing at about 8000 feet above sea level. The lookout point allowed a clear vantage to observe the shattering effects. The GoPro worked. I captured a six-minute video of the crater including walking back towards the base camp.

During the walk downhill, the snow had eased off, and it stopped completely by the time I was ready to leave. It was already 5:00 p.m. I was going to have to drive longer than I would have liked. My daily goal had been driving around four to five hours at the most per day.

As I exited the area and returned towards the road, I drove through some light rain. The highway led through a few different Indian territories. I was stopped at one checkpoint conducting a DUI search for drunk drivers. It was odd since it was so early in the evening. The landscapes were stunning. The cliffs and rock formations were fascinating. Especially with the clouds poised above them in ever-changing shapes. The clouds ranged from the normal white to shades of grey and black, perhaps indicating stormy weather approaching.

Without trying to sound disrespectful, as I drove through the different territories, I noticed immense pockets of poverty. The structures resembled each other. I observed minimal amenities around. While driving through the Zuni territory, I noticed they had some shops open for tourists to purchase items. The landscapes were spectacular through the Zuni land.

As time elapsed and the sun began to set on the horizon, I thought I might have to camp out along the road or perhaps locate a campsite. Every town I entered was small with nowhere to park and sleep in my truck safely. I passed a restaurant or a gas station but nothing else.

I continued driving along the blacktop two-lane road. I noted possible options where I could pull over on the side of the road, but I would not feel safe sleeping in such a situation. Another thing I had seen all day was local dirt roads branching off into the cliffs. I was curious to know what might have been down those roads. I continued to have faith I would arrive in a town with a Wal-Mart. And sure enough, when I reached the town on the map where I told myself I was going to stop, eat, and sleep no matter what, it had a Wal-Mart.

I was in Show Low, Arizona. Navajo County. It was established in 1870. I read the city was named based on a poker game.

The negative about the Wal-Mart was it offered no WiFi. It was the third one I had visited with no WiFi. I was used to all the Wal-Marts offering free WiFi, even in the parking lots. It was also located about ten minutes outside of the town, which was another odd thing. It was dark when I arrived. My cell phone was only 2G, so I couldn't search to find out if there was a Starbucks around. I researched the weather. The temperature was predicted to drop to 21 degrees overnight. It was the coldest night of the tour so far. I would soon see if it affected my ability to sleep. I asked myself if I might have to crank the engine for the heat at some moment during the night.

The truck had had a hard workout that day, with about six hours of driving and recharging all the devices. I'd had it idling for the past two hours with the heat on, creating a toasty warm interior as I wrote about the day's adventure.

The goal for the next day was Phoenix, Arizona. I planned to reconnect with a high school friend I had not seen in 25 years. The originally scheduled tour had me in San Diego, California already. I was over 500 miles behind. I was remaining longer in some of the cities because of the chance to perform. I drove slower than anticipated as well. Yet, I concluded, it was the correct way to move along instead of rushing through. I had about four and a half weeks remaining before I had to be in Mississippi for the 2016 Mississippi Music Foundation Awards Show.

APRIL 1, 2016

My mind drifted as I drove. I attempted not to worry about the how. I asked, I believed, and I had faith those things I desired would arrive. I knew it would happen in God's time and not mine. If it had happened in mine, I would already be a multi-millionaire with an EP selling over 50,000 copies and be a best-selling author. I continued to have patience and faith. Everywhere I looked, I saw the miracles of God.

I bundled up in clothes to turn in. With the sleeping bag wrapped around me. I knew I was being taught lessons on my journey. *God used solitude to teach us how to live with other people. God used rage to show us infinite value of peace. He used boredom to underline the importance of adventure and spontaneity. God used silence to teach us to use our words responsibly. He used fatigue so we could understand the value of waking up. He used illness to underline the blessings of good health. God used fire to teach us about water. He used earth to explain the value of air. He used death to show us the importance of life. I was truly grateful for Paulo Coelho for showcasing those lessons in his book* Warrior of the Light.

AZ-260-West
Arizona

CHAPTER 23
APRIL 2, 2016

I almost managed to make it through the entire night before becoming too cold inside of the truck. I awoke around 5:30 a.m. I had to crank the engine to heat up the truck. After twenty minutes, I turned the key off and returned to sleep for another two hours. I had slumbered well the past two nights. Vivid dreams along with minimal tossing and turning from side to side had helped. I might finally be adapting to the back seat of the truck.

As I was leaving Show Low, Arizona, I noticed a mountain bike trail to the right. I almost stopped, but it was only in the lower 30s. Rather, I decided to continue driving towards Phoenix. Besides, I wanted to arrive in Phoenix to connect with my old high school friend.

The drive for the day was beyond majestic. I perceived the hand of God while I was looking upon His landscapes. The expedition elevated to approximately 8000 feet. The downgrade was to 4000 feet. The bluffs and canyons were jaw-dropping. I paused at one turn-off spot to eat a snack, embrace the beauty, and snap a few pictures. The difficulty about driving through such exquisite country was wanting to stop every 5 minutes for pictures or simply to stand in awe.

The roads were curvy and cut through the landscapes like a serpent. Those roads were created at some point in our history. I thought about the people who had created them and the difficulty the complex designs required. Part of me was happy I could drive through the country. Yet, I was also saddened to notice the area was changed due to technology. Some of the bluffs were mind-blowing. Sadly, there were different types of towers on top of each bluff. I imagined observing the territory on horseback before the roads were ever created.

The small towns I went through had their founding dates posted on historic markers at the side of the road as one entered the city limits. Most were in the 1860s.

The area possessed numerous ranches. The cowboys and farmers installed barbed wire fences around them. Some of those ranches were over twenty-five miles along the highway. I was curious how far back they went.

I drove through more Indian territories as well. The most beautiful I had seen so far were the Navajo and Tonto territories. The only regret I had in passing through was observing a trailhead for mountain biking. I could have taken a break and seen some breathtaking scenery from a different perspective. I regretted not stopping for

APRIL 2, 2016

a ride. The trailhead might have had sights which I would never see again. I had allowed my inner voice to talk me out of stopping because I wanted to find a place to perform on the streets in Phoenix and visit my friend Jason.

One thing I learned on the tour was to attempt to quiet the EGO. The EGO was the inner voice creating the fear standing in my way. 'Take a chance,' I told myself. 'Take a risk. Enjoy the journey. Regret kills the soul."

I arrived in Phoenix, Arizona around 1:30 p.m. It was the capitol of Arizona. It was nicknamed the "Valley of the Sun." It was settled in 1867.

From what I had seen of the city so far, I liked it. There were lots of activities and things to do. It was almost 80 degrees, which meant their summers were in the 100s, which would not be too much fun. Phoenix residents tried to compensate for it with their old saying, "But it's a dry heat."

I browsed the internet to locate places to perform. An option was a bookstore in the arts district which sounded promising. Phoenix was supposed to be open-minded about street performers. No permits were needed to use an amp or to busk. I arrived at the bookstore; but, the owner was not present. Anyhow, the person there said it should be cool for me to perform somewhere out on the street tonight. Just in case, I walked and talked to people at about eight other businesses. Again, in most cases, the owners were not there. The store assistants all said the same thing, I should be okay, though, not to be surprised if I were hassled by the police. They told me the night before was their first Friday of the month, which meant about 15,000 people had walked through the area. Numerous street performers were set-up along the path. They said there may be some people walking around tonight. It seemed they were more lenient on first Fridays than on other evenings. I was told if the cops approached me, I would usually first be given a warning to leave. If I remained there when they came back, they would issue a ticket.

The spot where I was given permission to play was in a decent location. The arts district was primarily one street about four blocks in length. There were small cafes, bookstores and art shops lining each side of the street. The buildings were old houses decorated creatively with paint. I was not allowed to set up on the actual sidewalk. There were dirt patches between the street and sidewalk where I could establish myself. I was hoping the book store/smoke shop would offer permission to perform inside their quad area. There were no tables, but the quad area was a nice concrete patio. I was instructed by the bookstore assistant to return in a few hours when the owner would be present to ask about performing on their quad.

My high school friend Jason lived about 40 minutes away from the arts district. If I performed, I would not be able to see him until after I finished, probably well after 10:00 p.m. I was planning to set up around 6:00 p.m. and play about two to three hours. Though I would love for hundreds of people to walk by and donate to my cause, I really desired to spend time with my friend. I located a place in the arts district to sit and think about staying to play or leaving for my buddy's house. The one thought which remained on my mind was the lack of practice on the trip. I had thought practicing the guitar and learning new songs would be an easy thing to accomplish. However, when I arrived in a town, I tried to find a gym, locate a Starbucks, and then a Wal-Mart. I did not allocate time to simply sit down and practice. As I moved further West, I told myself, I would have more opportunities to camp, which should allow practice and composing time, as there would be no internet or other distractions. As my journey continued, it was evolving into more of a writing and sight-seeing trip instead of a busking tour. When I searched online to locate busking laws in each city I stopped in, the city ordinances were negative toward busking. The cities placed it in the same category as panhandling, identical to what the homeless undertake.

Superstition Mountains of Arizona

CHAPTER 24

APRIL 3, 2016

Last night, I returned to the Arts District in Phoenix, Arizona around 6:00 p.m. I paid for parking along a side street off the main drag of the Arts District. I noticed the streets were congested with cars: a good sign.

I returned to the bookstore. The owner was still not there. The girl inside said he would not be there for another hour. I went next door to the smoke shop and asked what time the guy they had mentioned earlier who performs on the corner usually set up. They told me he had a crazy side. If I were in his spot, he might yell or cuss me out, even though he was not there every night. He assumed it was his personal spot no matter what. They said he would set up right at dark, which was in about another hour. The other street corner I saw earlier in the day would work, but multiple shop owners had told me I may be hassled by the cops there.

After standing outside for about 10 minutes pondering my options, I decided to skip performing and went to visit my high school friend Jason. Besides, I reasoned, the NC Tar heels were playing on TV in the Final Four. Maybe we could watch the game together. Jason was from North Carolina. I moved there from Mississippi in the third grade. We became friends in the sixth grade.

So, I punched his address into the GPS and headed his way. I was surprised he lived so far away from Phoenix because his office was in the city. He had a long commute. As I was driving to his house, the gas light appeared. Being a guy, I told myself I could easily make it to his exit and get gas there. The gas light was on for roughly 10 miles when I exited. I noticed there were no gas stations. I had to turn around, drive back to the Interstate and drive another mile west until I located a station. I repeated prayers I would make it. When I pulled into the gas station, the truck required 18.1 gallons. I basically had an 18-gallon tank. I probably pushed the limits on that adventure!

When I arrived at Jason's house, it was dusk, but I still could see he had a very lovely home. It turned out to be over 4,500 square feet with a four-car garage. The house was located against a nature preserve, so no other houses were around him. His backyard had a pool with a Jacuzzi waterfall, and a separate area with a fireplace and love seats around it, all with the mountains of Arizona in the backdrop. Quite astonishing, I must say.

APRIL 3, 2016

We caught up and talked about what we had done since high school, which was interesting. I was introduced to his wife. We watched the NC Tarheels win the National Championship.

Since I was alone so much, the visit reminded me how valuable friendships were. It made me realize how I looked forward to having someone with whom I could share my future adventures with, and the importance of having a circle of friends who did things together along with shared activities.

The next morning, after a marvelous night's sleep in a king size bed and a hot shower, I departed for California to visit a friend in Oceanside. Oceanside was about 30 to 45 minutes north of San Diego. It was about a six-hour drive to the destination. I thought I might stop somewhere for a mountain bike ride before arriving at her house.

As I drove, the landscapes transitioned from flat to mountainous to desert, returning to mountainous and finally ending at the Pacific Ocean. I was surprised at the temperature since I had departed Arizona in the low 80s. As I was driving through El Centro, California, I noticed it was over 92 degrees outside. It was not common to have these types of temperatures on the East coast until later in the year.

I remained on Interstate 10-West for most of the trip after I left Phoenix. When I examined the Google Maps on my phone, I decided to leave the Interstate in Blythe and go onto Highway 78. It allowed for adventurous back roads to her house in Oceanside. It was a fantastic two-lane highway which steered me past sand dunes which I had only viewed in the movies. People were riding motorcycles, dune buggies, and trucks. It seemed one could simply pull off the road and head out onto the desert and do whatever one desired. I observed lots of RVs out on the desert and imagined they were probably using their ATVs to explore. I thought about stopping and riding my bike some, however, I was afraid to leave the truck in the middle of nowhere, knowing I had all my belongings inside.

I cruised on curvy roads into the mountains to about 4,000 feet then descended. The route passed through a great small town called Julian. It was flooded with tourists. The city was in the Cuyamaca Mountains and contained country stores, horse-drawn carriages, and multiple bed and breakfasts lining the streets. Many of the buildings on Main Street were built in the 1870s. It was only an hour away from San Diego.

I stopped along the way and captured pictures and videos of the stunning landscapes. It was probably the coolest road I had traveled on since I had relocated from Colorado in the early 2000s. There were countless curves and hills. I could smell my burning brakes by the time I finished the drive.

I stopped at one picnic area which had tremendous views from the picnic tables. I sat down to write, as I was feeling inspired. Unfortunately, the laptop battery was dead even though I had charged it the day before at a Starbucks.

As the evening closed in, I arrived in Oceanside. My friend Cheryl lived about three blocks away from the Pacific Ocean. We went out to dinner, then walked around the strand and down to the pier. People were out on the beach with campfires burning, something I had never seen on the East Coast. It was chilly. Later, we drove past a house which was used in the movie *Top Gun*. It appeared to be a keen little town. Everyone gave the impression of safety. Cheryl stated she was comfortable walking at night and was not frightened of something happening to her.

So, as you read this, you might understand why I changed the original title. Due to rarely performing, I did not believe the title should have remained, "A Country Boy Busking Across America." *Up to the current point, I had only busked two times on an actual street. Yet, I was blessed to be traveling this journey and seeing those sights. I wish the blessing upon you too!*

Relaxing on the sofa, I recalled recently watching *The Last Samurai*. A scene struck me like a lightning bolt. When Tom Cruise's character was practicing, a young Samurai told him, "no mind." I pondered the two words. I understood how many times we allowed our mind to get in our way. I could recall numerous points in my life of it occurring. Mostly seen in athletics: when I attempted to think too much, I would turn the basketball over or miss the crucial golf shot. When I was focused on the moment and let go, my body took over what I had practiced so many times before, which created success.

The above was a Zen expression. When your mind was not fixed or occupied by a thought or an emotion, it was free to excel. Our EGO creates nervousness and distractions. In a fictional movie with Kevin Costner, *For the Love of the Game*, his character could mentally block out the crowd to allow his arm to repeat what he had practiced a thousand times.

When you let go, you are free of anger, fear, or EGO. Our bodies become truly free to act. As I continued to change my life through dreaming big and listening to my heart, I saw how my own mind had gotten in the way. I had already allowed my mind to talk me out of multiple possible street performances and a few songwriter nights.

I was striving for mental clarity. A deeper awareness of enhanced perceptions. Some might call it the 'zone'. Others might have said a trance. As I continued reading about becoming a "Warrior of the Light," the above underlying themes were key. I was in awe knowing how powerful our minds are. Ponder for a moment the amazing things which have been created in our world originating from the mind.

I imagined by focusing daily to those standards, I could let go of the distractions surrounding me, operate from a state of clarity. I would become efficient. My goals, desires and dreams would manifest quickly.

Beach Volleyball Courts
Oceanside, California

CHAPTER 25
APRIL 4, 2016

I awoke to a foggy morning in Oceanside. I had stayed with my friend Cheryl the previous night. The plan was to remain on the sofa one or two more nights. When I could lodge with someone, stretched out, it reminded me how tired and fatigued I was. Even though I was not performing like I had originally planned, I guessed the combination of driving, writing, sight-seeing, and attempting to find places to play in each new city was taking a toll. I believed I would feel improved and have more energy if I had pre-planned the tour. It would have removed the unknown as well as added a guaranteed cash flow.

I researched the Oceanside area. Once again, busking/street performing seemed to be frowned upon. Oddly, the San Diego music scene was on a list of the top cities opened to street performing.

I cruised on my yellow mountain bike along the Pacific Ocean. I thought about stopping from time to time to ask shop owners about busking. Along the ride, I did read a flyer about a local open mic opportunity. It was not until Wednesday night, and I planned to leave before then.

The plan was to head toward Los Angeles the next afternoon. Once again, I told myself to perform on the street somewhere. From watching movies and online searches, I saw Venice Beach was the place to go for busking. I was on Venice Beach in the late '90s while traveling with the Florida A&M University Basketball team. We were on a California road trip playing a few games. I recalled Venice Beach covered with individuals selling trinkets or performing.

The weather was superb, in the high 60s. I toured for about ten miles around Oceanside. I looked for some street performers or a cop I could ask for information about busking. I never came across either.

Online, I contacted a musician in Seattle, Washington. He was a fan of Tommy Ray Music on Reverbnation. He was gathering information about performing in the Seattle area for me. It would be a couple of weeks or more before I was in Seattle. I was sticking to the goal of driving about four hours each day. I'd then stop, research options to perform, and find a place to spend the night.

While out at dinner with Cheryl, I spoke with a young lady whose boyfriend performed on the street from time to time in Oceanside. She told me every Thursday they closed a local street to have a festival. It would offer an opportunity to busk. She added an open mic also occurred on Thursday nights. She also mentioned in the summer time there were more street performers because there were more people visiting the area and it was warmer at night. She stated musicians typically set up near the pier.

Overall, Oceanside offered the possibility of a location I would enjoy living full-time. With San Diego so close, I could see every major musical and comedy act along with always having something interesting to do. The real estate there was affordable. The people appeared authentic and cordial. In addition, there were plenty of road trip options from one to four hours away.

I received a message from another ex-FAMU basketball teammate who lived in Los Angeles. He invited me to LA to catch up with him. I decided I would probably leave Oceanside the next day to head up the coast.

As the "Confessions of a Dreamer Tour" continued, I was leaning more to writing and open mic live musical performances than street performing. I sensed negativity about street performing. I wanted to remain positive and optimistic.

After Cheryl turned in for the night, I sat upon her sofa and thought. *What creates luck? Why does it seems with some individuals everything they touch turns to gold? Is it luck? When we fail, some people state they were "unlucky." Is luck a deception? On a website called* Changing Minds, *it stated luck causes us to hide our skill by saying we were just lucky. Due to the lack of skill, we use the excuse of being unlucky. When we fail at something, we blame it on being unlucky instead of ourselves. A major lesson learned through my teachings were to take responsibility for myself. Do not wish things are easier, wish I am better.*

I liked to think I was creating what I obtained through faith, hard work, diligence, and a positive attitude. With visualization, I knew it was on its way. I simply believed.

I laid my head on the pillow to close my eyes. I was truly grateful for the blessings bestowed upon me. I was living my dream. I was on tour, writing, and creating inspiration.

Long Beach, California

CHAPTER 26

APRIL 5, 2016

I made a mistake as I was leaving Oceanside. Before arriving, I had printed off venues offering open mics in the surrounding areas. I neglected to look at them after I arrived at my friend's house. I finally scanned those sheets of paper and realized I could have performed at an open mic from Sunday through Thursday nights. I remained positive, though, because I did not waste time in Oceanside. I decided it was an alluring city, and it was great to catch up with Cheryl.

The drive north along the coast was everything I expected. Two hours of relaxed beach communities filled with enticing prospects for future living. On the way north, I compared those different areas to Oceanside. I could see myself living in Oceanside based on its artistry, offered events, and the affordability. Besides, Oceanside conveyed the impression of a small, close-knit town. I thought if I ever chose to relocate to California, I would have to live as close to the ocean as possible. I would not enjoy being away from the coast. When I was away from the ocean, it was warmer and no different than any other East Coast area I have lived except more expensive. As I drove up the coastline. I believed it would be my philosophy anywhere in California.

Besides Oceanside, I delighted in Laguna, California. It was complementary to Oceanside, yet a bit more upscale with their stores and living accommodations.

Based on the map, the drive was two hours to Long Beach. Though, with the normal California traffic, I arrived in Long Beach after five hours of driving. It was a lot larger than I thought it would be. It had the appearance of a major city. With it already being late afternoon, I tried to decide where I should have a celebration dinner for coming so far. The only place which crossed my mind was the world-famous Roscoe's. I ordered the chicken and waffles platter. It was remarkably tasty and worth the time and money.

I was not able to connect with my friend Brian tonight. We had attended FAMU together in the late 90s and were on the basketball team together. Instead, I returned to the usual routine. I located a Starbucks to use their WiFi and enjoyed a cup of green tea with a dessert cookie. I researched venues to perform. I looked up the weather, as it looked like it might rain for a few days. Afterwards, I parked at a Wal-Mart to sleep. I examined the original travel plans I had created before leaving Mississippi. The initial planning had me in Portland, Oregon. I was 991 miles south of Portland, 15 and a half hours away.

Long Beach brought out thoughts of living in a big city. To accomplish the feat, it would take money. *We desire to be rich. We work long hours, gamble, play the lottery, steal, or hope for an inheritance from a lost relative. There are thousands upon thousands of books on how to obtain riches. We pray, ask God, and ask the Universe in attempt to manifest money.*

I do believe becoming rich assists in creating happiness. "You are rich if you have enough to satisfy all of your desires." My oldest brother desired to walk the Appalachian Trail for over 30-years. He continued putting it off because he stated it was too expensive. My middle brother owned his own company and could fish or hunt anytime he desired with the added benefit of being generous to the family. Experiences create happiness. The above might be my own personal point of view. The amount of money needed to add experiences to your life, to increase your generosity to others, seems priceless. It's up to you to figure out what is considered rich/wealthy.

Personally, for me, I desire to visit the world. To be able to touch, smell, taste, and observe the beauty God created. We are free to choose our own desires. I perceive there was an abundance surrounding all of us. If no one was hurt, neglected, or manipulated, go for what you desired no matter how many zeros are after the amount. Embrace your passions. We are only here a short time. Enjoy life intensely.

So, I leave it to you, my readers. No matter your choice, remain positive, act with love, and savor each breath. Someday, you will not inhale. Your time will end. I began my new path in May 2014 at the age of 41. When people ask me what I do now, I state, "I am a full-time author and songwriter." If I ever return to medicine, I may say it was my part-time job, no matter the amounts of hours I might have to work.

Look in the mirror. Make your decision. What do you consider rich? Do not have regrets, my friends. When you decide, train your mind. Pray, create a vision board, read, practice, remain faithful, trust you are already there. Believe your thoughts and create your reality. Be blessed. Be grateful. Be appreciative.

Made Storefront
Long Beach, California

CHAPTER 27

APRIL 6, 2016

It was a good day in Long Beach. I awoke early and began the day after a so-so night of sleeping in a Wal-Mart parking lot. I had continued hearing noises in the parking lot around me. When I awoke for the first time it was much earlier in the morning than I thought. It was 1:30 a.m. I eventually returned to sleep until 8:00 a.m.

The Wal-Mart was approximately 20 minutes outside of the popular streets of Long Beach. With the sun shining, I was surrounded by blue skies. I thought of visiting the Aquarium. The city of Long Beach was erecting structures for an upcoming Indy car race. A few of the streets were closed. The phone's GPS was malfunctioning, unable to direct around the detours. I became confused and crossed over a huge bridge. I ended up in the port area where the large ships were being loaded with cargo containers. I returned to the city. I chose another turn. The road was closed because they were shooting a movie. I saw a few actors in a car but did not recognize who they were.

I located a park with free parking across from the beach. I asked a gentleman if it was safe. He said it was safe during the daytime. The park offered a square where you could do weight exercises. There was also a skate park and a playground for little kids.

I hopped on my yellow mountain bike. I went on a 10-mile ride. I rode around the city, down onto the beach's boardwalk, and back. I traveled to the pier. They were preparing for a sailing race over the next few days. I watched the boats practice. They were having match races between two boats. I shot some videos of the boats which I planned to post on my YouTube channel. I was still figuring out the proper angles when I used the Go-Pro camera with the bike helmet.

After the bike ride, I parked near the Promenade. I walked around the busier streets to locate a place I could perform. I spoke to a person in a store, called Made. They stated it was cool to set-up outside their front door. I thanked them and told them I would return around 4:30 p.m.

I returned to the beach. I sat there for about an hour. The sand was spongy and delightful. The temperature was brisk, even though the sun was out. I sat in a folding camping chair, watching the barges in the distance and the birds playing around me. For lunch, I had a few street tacos with a soda. I continued enjoying the beach oasis, though, some irritating little bugs similar to gnats landed on me, which ruined the tranquil mood. The other negative part of the beach location was the public restrooms. The stall contained trash, dirty toilet paper, and a bloody shirt.

At 4:30 p.m., I parked at a public garage around the corner from the Made store. I transported the equipment by hand and set up on the street in front of the Made store sign. The owner or a person working in the store came outside and asked me if I wanted to put anything behind their counter for safety. The experience up to this point gave me the sense of how street performing should be. It was odd watching the cops ride by and not say anything to me. Almost everywhere else on tour, they would have stopped and told me to stop. I performed for about two and a half hours. I stopped before it got dark. I wanted to ensure I would return to the parking lot while it was still light outside. There was not as much foot traffic as I thought there would be. I only earned enough in tips to pay for parking. Yet it was still fun. I received the normal smiles, thumbs up, and a photographer even stopped and clicked some pictures. I sold one autographed EP.

After the busking experience, I located a Starbucks. I wanted to get caught up on all my social media accounts. I had to visit three separate Starbucks to locate one which had an open space to sit and charge devices. Ultimately,

I was waiting on my college friend, Brian from FAMU. I was supposed to catch up with him and crash at his place that night.

As I unpacked the devices, I noticed all the batteries were dead. They had not charged well inside the truck. Earlier in the day, I had sat in the truck over an hour with it on idle, attempting to charge the batteries.

Around 10:00 p.m., I finally heard from my college friend. After obtaining his directions, I drove to his place. It turned out to be on the main Ocean Boulevard. His balcony offered a perfect view of the Indy track from the eighth floor. He had one of the best views of the finish line you could ever ask for. He told me he had lived there for the past four years. He commented, after the first year, his excitement over the race wore off due to the loud noise created by the Indy cars. He mentioned they had multiple types of races once the track was set up, including an electric car race. The electric car race was his favorite, because the noise was not too disturbing. On race day for the Indy cars, the noise began around 9:00 a.m. It seemed not to stop until 9:00 p.m. The other days were nearly as loud leading up to the race for practice and qualifying. I laughed, knowing I had been able to drive on parts of the track the past two days, because it was made up of the normal streets of Long Beach. It was hard to believe they could drive 200 mph on normal streets.

APRIL 6, 2016

We visited for a couple of hours, but by midnight we were both tired. Brian woke up daily at 5:00 a.m. to beat the dreadful California traffic to his job, which was about 30 miles away. He also worked out at his gym before work every day. His commitment and dedication inspired me.

"I opened my heart to the Universe and asked God to give me the inspiration I need" –Paulo Coelho. Through faith, I was inspired to dream big. Through focus, visualization, and remaining positive, I sharpened my clarity. I did my best and let God worry about the outcomes. I released my expectations and trusted my creativity was my greatest power. I created value and inspiration for others.

Pacific Ocean Along HWY 1 North

CHAPTER 28
APRIL 7, 2016

When I awoke, I was grateful for the bed and shower. I did not know when I would have another bed to enjoy along the remainder of the journey. I had been able to sleep about four hours. I did not know exactly how far I wanted to drive now that I was awake. I was thinking the normal four to five hours at the most, then locate a Starbucks and a Wal-Mart. I had been told there might be places I could camp for free or very cheaply right on the beach as I traveled north up the Pacific Coast Highway. The thought brought a smile to my face.

As I cruised Highway 1 North, I noticed traffic already building. It was only 5:30 a.m., still dark, but all roads were bumper to bumper. I had another friend in Los Angeles, Ola, whom I was going to try and visit. He also said he left two hours before work to drive the 20-mile commute to make sure he arrived on time each day. I guessed it was common for the area.

As I continued north, I became aware the Pacific Coast Highway did not align directly along the shoreline like I had originally thought. At some points, I was forced to drive on the freeway.

Within the first 30 to 45 minutes of driving, I entered the Manhattan Beach area. I decided to stop at a parking lot along the beach to watch the sunrise. The morning air was chilly, with grayish overcast skies. Sun exposure there was limited, but I was able to watch the surfers and paddle boarders for about 10 minutes. They were all covered up in their wetsuits as the Pacific Ocean was frigid compared to the warm waters of the Gulf I was used to in Florida. There were special bike paths running parallel to the beach where one could ride. I was beginning to understand why so many people loved living along the California coastline. I could see myself living there as well.

I continued up the coast, surprised how far inland I was at times. As I approached LA, Highway 1 brought me under the airport. I could see the planes, like the ones for FedEx, taking off, right before my eyes.

I noticed as I continued north from Long Beach to LA the beach cities did not appeal to me as much as they did from Long Beach south to Oceanside. They had less charm and positive vibes. I thought to myself if I did choose to relocate to California someday, it would be from Long Beach south to the San Diego region as close to the coast as I could afford. I did not see any reason to relocate to California to simply live in the mainland, away from the ocean. Living away from the coastline would not create the same California positive, optimistic vibration for me.

Near Santa Monica, I returned to the true Highway 1 driving parallel the coastline. It was as stunning as I could have imagined. There were lots of turnoffs where one could stop to snap pictures or hike down to the beach and enjoy a picnic.

When I first reached Malibu, I did not understand all the hype I'd heard about the place. It didn't seem like somewhere the rich and famous would live. The city itself did not seem to offer enough of the things I enjoyed, like music, art, or cultural activities.

I noticed lots of campgrounds where one could stay for a nominal fee along the drive. I only saw one place on the highway allowing camping on the beach. Everything else was day-use only. No matter though; the scenery alone was well worth the slower pace.

I reached Santa Barbara and thought about two friends I had in Florida. My previous supervising physician, Dr. Mirabello, had a home there with his wife. They visited a few times a year. Another friend, Jim, who co-wrote my song, "Zama" with me, used to live there as well and played music. He had been a mentor, coach, and friend since 2009. Santa Barbara was a considerably larger city than I thought. It offered everything for art and music.

I stopped at a rest area in Gaviota, at the junction where I returned to Highway 1 from the freeway. I noticed a roadside marker for El Camino Real, which made me laugh considering how I resigned my position in orthopedic surgery in 2012 to travel to France and Spain to walk the Camino de Santiago, the Way of St. James,. I rested a short time and noticed they had rattlesnake warnings. Rattlers like to come down from the rocks in the summer and lay on the cool concrete. Thank goodness it was daytime and only in the low 60s. I was not a snake enthusiast.

After a while, I departed the rest area. The landscape transitioned into agricultural. There were fields of strawberries and other produce. I saw workers picking fruit and performing other tasks to aide with the harvest. I thought about my Uncle James who lived in my hometown of Zama, Mississippi. Having the knowledge to plant a seed, to know when to plant, and then to harvest a crop one can consume was almost becoming a lost art in our country. Humans are amazing. We created tractors and invented machines to harvest crops faster than a field full of human pickers could do. Then it was sent to processing centers and factories where technology was utilized to dehydrate or freeze the crop, or even transform it into a ready-to-eat meal.

When I drove, I either listened to some motivational tapes or nothing at all; I simply enjoyed the scenery. My thoughts drifted in amazement at the creation of the highway itself. It would have been interesting to see the area without the asphalt roads. I wondered when those roads were constructed. Was the road I was traveling on the original road, or had it been updated over the decades, or centuries even? I had similar thoughts about the power lines. I was in awe of the curves and of whoever had designed the highway in the first place. How did they know to bend the road here or there?

I started to look for potential places to stop for the night. I continued looking at the map. I wanted to see what Grover Beach or Pismo Beach offered. In my mind, I was still thinking Starbucks and Wal-Mart. I noticed my cell phone had no service since leaving LA. I saw no place to stay unless I wanted to pay for a hotel room or perhaps a campground.

I continued driving. I watched the miles and the hours tick by, and the gas being used up. The next stop was Morro Bay. I originally drove past Morro Bay to see what the next city only a few miles up the coast had to offer. But my curiosity brought me back to Morro Bay because there was a huge rock in their harbor which I wanted to see. As I drove into the small fishing town, I realized it was an interesting little port. I noticed a music store on their main street. I told myself after visiting Morro Rock, I would go back to the store. As I entered the area by the Rock, I saw Morro Bay was larger than it first appeared. It offered a lot of interesting shops for tourists. The main drag near Morro Rock had lots of bars and restaurants.

I parked by the big rock and saw one could drive around it. I remained in the parking lot viewing small sailboats and kayakers. I noticed a young sea lion playing by itself in the water. It was floating around on his back making clapping noises. I watched him play around for about ten minutes before heading back to the music store.

When I entered the music store, I was greeted by the owner. We briefly spoke about the "Confessions of a Dreamer Tour." He had a few clients, so I walked around to check if there were any left-handed guitars I could play. Like most music stores, they had none. After his clients were gone, we talked further about the tour. He told me there was a restaurant near Morrow Rock which might let me play some music. In exchange, they might provide me something to eat along with some tips. After shaking hands and saying thank you, I returned to the restaurant. Unfortunately, someone was already setting up to perform for the small crowd.

I jumped into the truck and headed north, thinking each new town ahead would perhaps provide a place to spend the night. After departing Morro Bay, the trip became more astonishing. Highway 1 North mutated into a snake of 20 mph curves uphill and down around blind bends with pull offs offering photo opportunities one could only dream of.

After the highway leveled out a bit, I saw a campground. I stopped in to ask how much it was for a night as a tent camper. The price was $20, which seemed expensive to

APRIL 7, 2016

sleep in the backseat. I inquired about a location on the map called "Sand Dollar," which allowed free camping. The attendant was unaware of it. She told me she once found a sand dollar at the beach. I smiled at her, returned to the truck and made a U-turn, moving north on Highway 1.

I noticed the low gas warning light appeared. Luckily, a station came into view along the snake. Due to its location, the gas price was $6 a gallon. Gas had been only $2.59 a gallon at the stations I had passed before. However, with the combination of the warning light and being still at least an hour to Monterey, I decided to add about 4 gallons, almost $25.

A few miles after obtaining fuel, I paused on a turn-off next to the road to snap pictures of the beauty surrounding me. Not only did the Pacific Ocean blow me away with its waves crashing against the rocks, but on the other side of the road were mountains covered in green grass with fog upon their horizons. The landscape was like photos I'd seen from Ireland or Scotland.

I came across a pull-off where stopping allowed a view of elephant seals lounging on the beach. It was low tide. There were hundreds of those huge elephant seals sleeping on the beach. I had my binoculars and could observe some playing in the water. I thought there were probably a few great white sharks around with a hungry appetite. There were also signs stating do not feed the squirrels. Those intelligent squirrels would approach you, sit on their hind legs like a dog and beg for some food. They were quite tamed. I wanted to break the rules just to see what they would do with a few bites of food, but I obeyed the signs.

A little way up the road, I noticed a pull-off offering a restroom with picnic tables. It was about 5:00 p.m. I thought I would make some dinner and write. I had been observing breathtaking views of the Pacific to enhance my creative energy. I met two young guys who were grilling at a picnic table. They were from the area. I asked them about areas offering free camping. I was blessed to discover there were some only two miles up the road. They gave me the directions. I headed there with excitement.

It was a right-hand turn-off from Highway 1. It was a twisting and barely two-lane road up into the hills above the ocean. Supposedly, at the top of the road was a campground. Along the way up were pull-offs where one could park and camp out. The road itself was 11 miles to the top. Yet, at 10 miles per hour, it took over 40 minutes to reach it. I spotted a location halfway up which looked out over the Pacific Ocean. Whoever was there last had even built a fire pit and wall. Nevertheless, due to the current drought, there were signs stating no fires were allowed unless one possessed a permit. I had no idea how to obtain a permit. I settled into the spot, thinking I might still make a fire to add to the ambience. The view was gorgeous. The Pacific Ocean was about 1,500 feet

APRIL 7, 2016

below me. The sun was setting over the west, with those green-covered mountains as the backdrop. The Universe had answered my request to camp for free and provided an astonishing view as a bonus.

As I sat in a red camping chair gazing out at the view, I wrote in my journal. As the sun was setting over the Pacific Ocean, a gentleman walked up. He was camping about a quarter mile above me. It turned out he was from North Dakota, also traveling around the country. We laughed, because today I had driven almost 300 miles, he had only driven 25 miles and just 20 miles the day before.

We talked about a lot of different subjects for about two hours until it darkened. I did not read or play the guitar like I had planned, but the conversation was quite welcomed. He invited me for some breakfast in the morning.

After he departed, I made dinner. I heated up the Panda Express black pepper chicken and rice, with a can of spaghetti with meatballs. I added cashews and almonds for dessert.

I did not have a lantern. I had to sit in the truck working on the journal after dark with the headlamp. I attempted it outside. Unfortunately, California also had flying insects. I thought about a campfire. Yet I was aware of the current law. I also understood the fire even in its pit could be seen from a distance. Another negative aspect was the sky was cloudy with no stars. As the darkness increased, the sounds of nature started their orchestra. The noises stirred nervousness within me. Nature's melodies created the perception someone was around the truck, circling it. But I knew I was safe. I had my gun with the doors locked.

I voiced my prayers of gratitude for safety, and in addition, for the amazing trip with its beautiful scenery. I had never seen anything like it in my entire life. The location I was in was simply a miracle from God.

It was pitch black at almost 9:00 p.m. A few cars were climbing up the winding road. I was surprised; I thought maybe the site was a hidden secret even though three cars passed. I was parked about 20 feet off the road. The spaces did not allow much room. Every time a car approached, their headlights shone into the truck. The optical illusion was of them about to drive straight into me.

We are all powerful. We all have minds which can generate miracles. We all have the minds to create anything and everything. We all have the key to our dreams. Unfortunately, some misplaced the key somewhere and stopped looking for it. Searching for our key is hard. It might be risky. You might be scared of what you must go through to find it. Yet, I like the pursuit. I live by the motto of "what if." What if someone read my book, loved it, purchased it, and shared it with someone else? Tommy Ray Books would grow. What if someone listened to my music? What if it inspired them to dream big and listen to their heart? What if? I would rather pursue the 'what if' than be at an older age with regrets. Regrets kill your soul.

Free Camping Site Along the Pacific Coast Highway
California
Pacific Ocean

Highway 1 North
California

CHAPTER 29

APRIL 8, 2016

I awoke numerous times throughout the night. I was jumpy, hearing sounds like someone or something was pacing around the truck. I exited the truck a couple of times with my gun and flashlight to check the surroundings. The fear was only in my mind. I talked to myself out loud, wishing for sunrise. At some point, I drifted back to sleep, and morning arrived. When I finally roused, I decided to make a small fire. It was for ambience and not for heat or cooking. The morning air was engulfed in a foggy mist. It was either originating at the ocean or out of those green fields above. The fog camouflaged the smoke coming out of the fire pit. As the flames ignited, I searched for the truck lock bed key. I thought I had lost it the night before when I checked the surroundings. I had combed the ground for it with a flashlight in the darkness. Unfortunately, I could not find it. Again, in the morning, I scoured the ground and under the truck. I removed everything from the backseat, passenger seat, but to no avail. I couldn't locate the key. It was the second time I had misplaced those keys. I boiled water in a small pot using the butane stove. I brewed hot tea and ate a simple breakfast of cashews, almonds, and peanut butter. On the floorboard, I discovered a can of pineapple juice. It was quite tasty. I drank pineapple juice before I sang as the juice lubricates your throat.

After consuming the tea, I used the remaining hot water to wash my face. Due to privacy concerns, I stood next to the truck as I took a quick sponge bath. I washed my hair with dry shampoo and shaved. I dressed in fresh clothes.

The fog and mist continued rolling in from the ocean. At times, it created the illusion the Pacific Ocean was invisible. My new friend camped above me would also be visible one moment and then hidden behind the fog a few moments later.

As I repacked, I checked my front blue jean pocket. Behold, there was the lock key. I was truly grateful I continued finding it. I did not recall wearing those jeans last night. I thought I was wearing Nike warmups the entire time. Nevertheless, I found it again after thinking I had lost it. I was truly grateful for the small blessing.

As I pulled away from the camping location, I wished I had more food. If I had, I would have stayed another night since I had not read any nor played my guitar thanks to sharing a conversation with my new friend the previous night. It was well worth it. I thought it was welcoming to having companionship from time to time. I was able to speak with him again in the morning and obtain his phone number. We were headed the same direction, though I was driving 200 to 300 miles per day. He was driving about 50 miles per day or less.

I searched the map to explore the possible route ahead. I was excited to see another free camping area ahead. It was about one to two hours north. I figured if I could find a store to obtain supplies, I would stop and catch up on reading and guitar practice.

As I drove up Highway 1 North along the coast, I was ecstatic it continued to curve around the shoreline. The speed limit was 25 mph on those two-lane roads. It was possible to take in a lot of the scenery, even as I was driving. I paused a couple of times to savor the moment and to take pictures. Most of the pictures of interest were from an area where a humongous rock seemed to be exploding up through the water with waves crashing around it.

As I approached the Bixby Creek Bridge, I noticed the turn-off for the free camping area. Sadly, it did not resemble a road…it was more like a dirt trail. It even had a sign stating the road was impassable if wet. A construction crew was working. I realized it was better to continue moving forward. I maintained unwavering faith another splendid and free location would appear.

I arrived in Monterey. It was a larger city than expected. I could have stopped and researched the possibility of performing either on the street or at a bar. However, it was Friday, and most open mic situations were only from Sunday through Thursday. Monterey offered a Wal-Mart to obtain supplies. I took a break for lunch and used their WiFi. I updated my social media and email. Twenty-four hours had passed without phone service. I was astonished at the amount of emails I'd received, though it was mostly junk and Facebook updates. The WiFi was powerful enough to upload pictures and videos to Facebook and Twitter. The content was an update about how the "Confessions of Dreamer Tour" was advancing.

I paused to think. *I was truly blessed and grateful. I was pursuing my desires and dreams, which meant I was successful. I wanted to travel the world, write about it, and have individuals purchase my books to read. In return, I wanted to inspire them to travel, even if simply to the next city.*

The Wal-Mart in Monterey had signs prohibiting overnight parking, something I had not noticed at any other Wal-Mart locations along the tour. Nor did they offer WiFi, a common occurrence since leaving Texas. Before I departed the Wal-Mart parking lot. I scanned the map trying to locate a campground. I'd be willing to pay if it offered captivating ocean views, amenities, and maybe some bike riding areas. The plan was to be somewhere by 1:00 p.m. I aimed to have enough time to relax, have some fun, and ensure I caught up with my reading and

APRIL 8, 2016

writing before darkness fell. Online, the Wilder Ranch State Park appeared to offer the above desired amenities. Wikipedia stated the Wilder Ranch State Park was a California State Park on the Pacific Ocean coast north of Santa Cruz. The park was formerly a dairy ranch. Many of the ranch buildings had been restored for use as a museum. When I arrived, it was only a day park. There was a ranger at the Park's gate. I asked about somewhere free to camp, along with advice about remaining safe. He was not able to guarantee safety, but he stated it was okay to park in the pull-offs along Highway 1 and spend a night or two there.

I departed the park and continued north. I drove across a bridge which a lot of surfers used for parking their cars. They walked across the road down to the beach to surf. I asked one of them about parking overnight. He referred me to some locations where he had camped. Unfortunately, when I checked them out, they were already filled with cars. So, over the next two to three hours I drove up and down the Pacific Coast Highway searching for the perfect spot to offer me a feeling of safety and a stunning view.

In that section of the PCH, there were multiple state parks. They offered astounding views. Yet I wanted a campsite for free. I continued to notice on the Highway 1, the pull-offs all had man-made dirt mounds blocking the ocean views when parked. I did not know if it was for safety reasons or to force tourists to pay $8 to use the state parks. I also realized the $8 payment was on the honor system, as none of those day parks had attendants.

I chose to go to the Butano State Park for camping. Per Wikipedia, Butano State Park was a state park showcasing a secluded redwood-filled canyon. Located in San Mateo County near Pescadero, the 4,728-acre park was established in 1955. The ranger recommended it highly. It was located on the opposite side of the ocean into the woods. I steered up and down a lengthy and twisting road. The route reminded me of the previous night. I was excited that I was finding a treasure. Unfortunately, none of the pull-offs offered interesting views. When I arrived at the ranger station, I learned it was $35 to camp overnight. Since I was sleeping in the back of the truck, I decided not to. I asked about places to sleep for free. She stated the same thing. Locate a pull-off I loved. I decided I would be okay for a night or two.

When I departed, my mission to locate the perfect spot continued. I drove another 40 to 60 minutes north trying out pull-off locations. At each site, something was missing. Either too close to the main road or perhaps a limited ocean view. After pausing at multiple areas, I finally said, "I am done." Of course, the last site was the finest. It was a quarter of mile from a state park which was located on the ocean. It was a grand pull-off. I was protected from oncoming traffic. The pull-off offered a walking path upwards to a ledge overlooking the open beach with a 240-degree view of the ocean with breaking clean waves. I set up the camping chair. I was surrounded by brush and blooming flowers. I could see the remnants of other people's stuff who had sat here before because the area was cleared out and there were some rocks piled up there. I placed the little butane burner on one of the rocks. I boiled water to heat a few hot dogs for dinner.

I considered sleeping outside. However, as I sat in the chair, I noticed a tick on the laptop as I was using for writing. Besides, it was a lot cooler there than it had been the previous night. I remained on the ledge bundled up as I listened to the waves and peered at the beauty God had created as I wrote. When I looked down, there were four different places the waves were breaking on the shore. They appeared to be perfect waves to learn to surf. The only thing was the water there was only about 60 degrees. I was spoiled from living in Florida, on the Gulf of Mexico, for a few years. I was used to the water temperatures being in the 90s.

As the sun set over the Pacific Ocean, a spectrum of colors was created. A misting rain began. A heavy fog rolled in. It forced me to retreat to the backseat of the truck.

It was Friday. The agenda for the next day was to arrive in San Francisco. Saturday and Sunday would be excellent days to perform on the street at the Wharf in San Francisco. The only thing I could not do was research the laws about busking with the street amp. The cell phone remained out of service.

As night approached, I wished the traffic would die down. It was quite busy through the section of Highway 1. The speed limit was 55 mph with numerous commuters on it compared to sections I had driven up to prior.

Try something different today. Even if it was choosing a different route home from work. Walk backwards to watch the world from a new perspective. Learn how to break down your barriers. Untangle your knots. Trust in yourself. Have faith in God, He will guide you properly.

Ledge Overlooking Pacific Ocean
Pacific Coast Highway

Alcatraz
San Francisco California

CHAPTER 30
APRIL 9, 2016

I was not hassled last night sleeping near the state park. I slept so completely; nature did not provide the same noises as the night before. The traffic lessened around 9:00 p.m., creating a peaceful evening. The melody of rain heightened around 9:30 p.m. The rain drowned out the crashing waves from below. One couldn't go wrong sleeping to the resonance of rain.

When I awoke, I placed a towel over the driver side window and opened the driver's passenger door with a towel over its window. It shaped a private area so I could wash off with the camping wash wipes and dress. I boiled hot water on the Butane burner to wash my face, shave, and brush my teeth.

I departed the area a little after sunrise. I was excited, knowing San Francisco was on the horizon. What I did not know was the rain and fog would continue all day long. The drive was not as majestic leading up to San Francisco as what I had seen so far. Nonetheless, it was still delightful.

Beginning 20 minutes outside of San Francisco, the fog thickened. I could only see about one car length in front of me. What surprised and even shocked me was most people were not driving with their lights on. I thought it was a law or simply being a responsible driver to ensure one could be seen as one drove through rainy, foggy conditions. I thought having good visibility was especially important on those curvy roads I was on. Highway 1 became four lanes instead of two. Yet it was treacherous driving with numerous blind curves. The only way I saw a stoplight ahead was from the huge flashing lights and sign about 100 yards before the light itself. The fog was so dense I could not read the street signs. There was a point where Highway 1 turned inland but Highway 35 remained along the shore. Since I was blinded by the fog, I accidentally turned onto Highway 35 south for about 10 minutes. Luckily, I saw the highway sign and did a U-turn.

I had no phone service for the past two full days. I thought perhaps the bill was past due or maybe there was a problem with the service. Once I turned around and headed north again, I located a Starbucks. I checked on the phone problem using their free WiFi to call T-Mobile. I required the phone primarily for the GPS. I utilized the laptop/iPad to post to social media accounts. The problem was at some point over the past two days, I had somehow turned off the data plan. Once I switched it back on in the phone settings, the phone worked perfectly again.

After solving the phone issue. I entered my desired destination into the GPS program. It was a public park which had a lighthouse with possible free camping. It was linked with the U.S. Department of the Interior of the Golden Gate National Recreation area. It was Fort Cronkhite. The directions traced the same route I had just been on. I guess being half-blinded from the rain and fog I had driven in a large circle. Once the GPS was working, I headed toward the destination. The route to the lighthouse passed by the zoo and returned to the coastline. What excited me the most was crossing the Golden State Bridge for the first time ever. Unfortunately, due to poor visibility from the fog, I couldn't see much as I traveled over the bridge. On the other side of the bridge was a rest area to stop and take some pictures. I could see places like Alcatraz in the distance. When I walked around the rest area, I had to use the umbrella carefully because of the high winds. Even with being extra cautious, the umbrella turned inside out a couple of times.

I exited the rest area and located the free camping area. I learned to obtain a spot, one had to call in advance for reservations. They had one location open, but one had to hike into the woods almost four miles to reach it. So, back into the silver horse I went and headed north again.

On the road atlas, I noticed another free camping site another hour north. Once again, I was on the twisting and curvy roads, climbing in elevation at 15 mph. The only problem was the wretched weather. I could not see anything due to the heavy fog. I slowly and carefully followed the route until I reached Stinson Beach. I turned onto another snake-like road which took me into a redwood forest for about 30 minutes. When I reached the top, there was a campground filled with trails on which I could walk or ride my bike. Once again, the only campsites available were the ones one had to hike into the woods to reach. Normally I would be cool with it, but it wasn't a great situation when I was sleeping in the back seat of the truck. Instead, I was off again. I headed further north.

I persisted in good spirits, not filled with anxiety or stress. I thought, "Okay, I will just find another pull-off area and enjoy an evening with a great view." What I did not know was I was in Sonoma territory. It was not allowed. Most of the pull-offs had signs stating no camping or sleeping in one's car overnight. Nonetheless, there were still a few without the signs. I even pulled into a few and contemplated staying. But my inner voice said, "No, keep going, it's not worth the hassle or possibly getting a ticket." Besides, the area was more residential.

APRIL 9, 2016

About every 10 to 15 miles I approached another small coastal town. Those towns had little restaurants and inns. I checked the prices online. They ranged from $130 - $250 a night. When I searched Hotels.com to locate a room, the cheapest was more than $85, and those were 20 miles inland with only fair ratings. I kept moving forward.

I stopped at one campground. Their cost was $35 a night. I thought it was a crazy amount to pay when I was sleeping in my truck. They told me about a campsite further up the road charging just $26. I kept pushing forward.

The section of Highway 1 North after the campground was interesting. It offered curvy roads overlooking fascinating views of the Pacific Ocean. Thankfully, due to the curves, I was driving at slow speeds. When I entered one sharp curve with a blind view, cows were crossing the road. I had to stop briefly to allow a calf and its mom to cross the highway and climb the hill. A doe was standing in the middle of the road around another curve a few miles later.

Finally, the road brought me to the Oceanview Campground. For $26, I could pick my spot, have a fire and take a hot shower. When I pulled into the campground, all the ocean slots were taken. Instead, I located a somewhat secluded spot about 400 yards from the ocean. But I noticed the people at one campsite were packing up. I walked over and asked about their spot. The man, whom

I assumed was the husband/father of the group, told me they were leaving. I must say the father did not look happy about it. Either the wife or two kids did not want to stay. It was 7:00 p.m. Darkness occurred at 7:45 p.m. I thought it was an odd time to leave a campsite. As soon as they vacated, I relocated my truck into their location. Unfortunately, I discovered it was all muddy. I was positive I would soon be getting mud on everything. On the other hand, the view made it well worth it. There was a walking trail down to a sandy cliff beach by the location, which was a great bonus. I did not have to rush out of there in the morning. I could do some hiking before departing. Unfortunately, there were no places to mountain bike, but a walk down to the beautiful beach seemed like a tremendous idea.

By 8:10 p.m., I was sitting along the side of the ocean. The evening temperatures dropped into the low 50s. A cold night was in store, even though the fire pit was blazing. I opened a beer. I relaxed into the camping chair, smiling. I had meant to play some guitar, but the rain began. There went my plan. The rain forced me to return to the truck for shelter.

Listening to the rain fall upon the truck, I closed my eyes as my mind rambled.

I have faith in you, my reader. There was magic in your life. Your plan might not happen overnight. It might take years, but so be it. Just try. I was cut from the basketball team my 6th – 11th grade years, made the team my senior *year, hardly played. Six years later, I was on a Division One Basketball team as a graduate assistant practicing. I was almost approved to play the year we went to the NCAA's to play against Duke.*

Walk through the closed door no matter how scary it may seem. Simply imagine. You never know unless you try. I jumped from an airplane at 13,500 because I had a $10 coupon. Though I may never do it again, I tried. I found out for myself if I loved it or hated it. Be the best version of yourself. Always remember, anything was possible. Believe in yourself. Have an open heart. The time was now. You are here.

Pacific Ocean
The Pacific Coast Highway

CHAPTER 31
APRIL 10, 2016

As I fell asleep last night to the tone of the Pacific Ocean, a few things about the day before popped into my mind. The first major notion was I had not stopped in San Francisco to attempt to perform. When I arrived in the city, it was cold and rainy. I stopped at a Starbucks to research the Wharf where I desired to perform. However, the spots which were designated for street performers required a permit which cost $50 per month or $500 for the year. My research suggested there were other locations to perform without a permit. Yet they were first come, first serve. A few comments mentioned one could be hassled by the police or other performers. Because of the stormy weather, I had never researched what was required to use a street amp while performing. When I was last at the Wharf about four years prior, the only street performers were mimes who were covered in paint and stood frozen like statutes, never making a sound.

Additionally, I researched singer and songwriter venues in the San Fran area. I located a venue. Unfortunately, I could not perform until Monday night. Because of the poor weather and being about 1,000 miles south of the original planned locale for the date, I moved forward north up the coast.

The previous night I had tossed and turned some. It was not related to any noises around me. I had numerous dreams come and go. After each little dream, I woke up. Yet, I was not able to recall any of them. I would reposition and fall back to sleep.

When I awoke in the morning, I started another fire, though it was mostly smoke. The dampness from the night before along with the mist continued. Due to the morning rain, I packed up more quickly than I had planned. The weather changed my plans to take the hike down to the beach. Even though it was misty, I prepared scrambled eggs for breakfast on the butane stove. After the preparation, I sat inside the truck to eat.

After the meal, I took a shower. The campsite offered a coin-operated shower. It cost $2 for about five to eight minutes. I was pleasantly surprised when the water was hot. There was no roof. It drizzled on me as I showered. Nonetheless, it was a hot shower, where I could wash my hair and my muddy flip flops.

April 10, 2016

As I began north from the starting point of Jenner, California, Highway 1 became much more residential. The roads curved away and to the ocean. The day's drive offered some flashbacks to New Mexico. The trip took me by sheep ranches. The grass was luscious greens with fields filled with sheep. I also noticed even with houses around, I still had no phone service with T-Mobile. The service would pop on for a quarter of mile, then disappear. I was slightly downcast when I realized I had missed a waterfall originating from the cliffs which fell into the ocean. It was in the Point Reyes region.

The first stop of the day was in Manchester. I located a McDonald's. I usually try to stay away from fast food, but their free WiFi was a major bonus. I used the opportunity to post on social media as well as e-mail. I also thought it was time to call my Mom and my Aunt Jo to let them know all was well. I realized I had forgotten to pay some bills which I needed to do the next day. I looked over paperwork to ensure I was not missing any sights. I definitely wanted to visit the Glass Beach, which was in Fort Bragg, California.

From what I gathered from the internet, Glass Beach was covered with thousands of pieces of broken glass washed onshore. Due to the water constantly washing over the glass, the pieces eventually transformed into smooth jewel-like translucent pebbles which were safe to handle because all the sharp edges had been worn off by the water. The photographs on the internet revealed all different colors and shapes of glass people scavenged for to create bracelets and necklaces.

When I first arrived in the area, I thought I was in the wrong location. The surroundings which the GPS on the phone was displaying were not the same. Fort Bragg turned out to be a normal town with lots of things in it, including a 4G network. I went against the GPS and located a parking spot. I walked a dirt path to the coast. There were lots of walking trails, but no access down to the beach. When I had researched it earlier, the information I found stated it was inside the MacKerricher State Park. So, I departed where I was and headed about four miles out of town. When I entered the park, the ranger said no, Glass Beach was back where I had been. I turned around and headed back into town. I parked at the little park there. I walked to the cliffs again and looked downward. I did not see anything. Nothing like the pictures online of a beach covered in jewels. I only stayed a short while and thought about the next move. I had seen another small parking area with restrooms about a mile before where I was. I adventured to the location. Behold, Glass Beach. I followed the people walking towards the beach and looked down upon the sand from the rock ledge I was standing on. It did not resemble the photographs. I noticed people picking up the colored glass. I probably remained 20 minutes before returning to the truck.

Before leaving the area, I'd discovered through research Fort Bragg offered a lot of mountain biking. I wondered whether to stay in the state park or get a hotel. If I remained in town, I could get a little dirty on my bike. It was only about 1:00 p.m. The state park's website didn't provide any campsite prices. I returned there, only to find out it was $35 to camp overnight. A steep price considering I was sleeping in my truck. The ranger did tell me of a state park about 20 minutes up the road was only $26. You guessed it: I went north.

As I twisted and turned around the 15 mph curves, I contemplated stopping in a pull-off for the night. I saw a couple of very large pull-offs which made one almost invisible to drivers on the main road. What kept me from stopping was no matter how I positioned the truck, I could see a residential home. I thought the proximity to an occupied house would make it more difficult when I had to use the bathroom or give myself a bath in the morning.

About five miles before the Westport-Union Landing State Beach, where I knew I could stay. I noticed a private campground with on-the-beach camping and other spots. When I originally walked in, I was given a price of $42. When I said thank you, but no thanks, the attendant asked me how many people were in my party and how many nights I planned to stay. I told her it was just me and I was sleeping in my truck. She gave me a new price of $25. I thanked her but moved forward, as I had been told about a state park where one could camp out above the Pacific Ocean on the bluffs. I was thinking what marvelous views those must be.

When I arrived, it was self-pay. It required cash which I did not have. Besides, it offered no showers or restrooms. It was basically an open field on top of the bluffs with no privacy. I turned back around and returned to the private campground.

At the private campground, I located a secluded site near the back of the campground. It bordered a flowing stream which was crystal clear. It led out to the ocean. There was one motorhome about 100 yards away. I parked the truck in a fashion offering some privacy. Besides, there was a line of small trees to separate the campsites. I purchased some firewood and a beer from their store. Another night I was paying to sleep. The original plan had been to spend every night in a free location. I spent a total of about $35 for the campground. The cheaper hotels were $70 a night in the area, with only fair ratings. There were lots of bed and breakfasts along with hotels offering fireplaces, hot tubs, and other romantic amenities. I was becoming quite self-sufficient. I saw no need to pay over $100 for a room when I had re-arranged the truck, allowing an almost fully stretched out position in the back seat.

I rode my bike to the beach through the campground. The sand was a blackish color. It had an unusual texture. It looked hard packed until you walked on it, then you sank into it. My footprints were a few inches in depth. It resembled gravel. I sat upon a boulder. When the waves crashed in, the run-off water surrounded the rock around

APRIL 10, 2016

me. I used the GoPro to capture video of it. The area where the stream entered into the ocean was not too far away. I walked over to see one little minnow swimming. As I mentioned earlier, the water was crystal clear; it looked clean enough to drink. I wondered if it was fresh water leading into the ocean, salt-water, or brackish.

Darkness occurred in about two hours. It was another overcast evening. There was no true sunset visible over the Pacific. I returned to the camping site to prepare for the night. The temperature was dropping quickly. I bundled up again with a headband, gloves and jacket. At dusk, I ignited the fire. I sat in the small red camping chair to access WiFi. The campground offered two free hours on each device. I planned to upload to Facebook a video I created about my music. I broke out my guitar and drank a beer while the fire crackled. The fast-moving stream in the background added to the soothing ambience. It was a great location to sleep outside. Unfortunately, I knew I would be bitten by bugs, and sleeping on the ground on a tarp curled inside a sleeping bag would not make me feel comfortable. I was safer in the truck. If I ever went tent camping, I would purchase a tent which would fit in the bed of a truck. I would like to be off the ground, so critters could not get in, especially if I left the tent door unzipped accidentally.

I had probably driven 150 miles today, if my calculations were correct. Normally, it was about two and a half hours of driving. Yet, driving 15 – 30 mph, it took more like four to five hours, especially when I wanted to pause and click pictures of all the beauty.

According to the road atlas, I would have to leave the coast to return to the 101 Freeway for a while. There was a road on the atlas following the coast, though it did not have a name. There were state parks listed on the road. I assumed it had to be a decent road to take, without any dangers. There were pictures of free camping sites along the road as well. I thought I might check them out. However, the ranger at the campground I spoke with did not recognize them when I showed him the atlas. The free campsite website has not been much help either. It listed sites 150 miles away from me or sites already behind me. When I read the details about the free campsites, most of them were glorified parking lots. I figured for the rest of the trip north to Seattle, I might have to stay in campgrounds each night or at the occasional hotel. The only way I could stay in a Wal-Mart parking lot was to go inland, which would remove me from all the charms of the Pacific Ocean.

As I looked over the road atlas, I realized I would reach Eureka, California, the next day. There were some things there I wanted to see. Even though it was only 90 miles from where I was currently sitting, I might spend the night there. Eureka could also perhaps provide a place to perform, like an open mic.

I had decided I should make the trip again in the future. The next time, I would begin up north and head south. It would also be a bonus if I had a passenger. They could look out their window and observe everything. Heading north, a passenger would not get to see everything due to the angles. I would also like to stop often and hike the trails and get in more mountain biking.

Before turning in, I stared into my crackling fire of red, blue and green hues.

The time was now. Life was a journey. My destination was death. Until then, I desired to be adventurous. My goal was to use my life to create inspiration and value to others. I have faith I can inspire others to listen to their heart, trust their instincts and chase big dreams. In return, they will inspire others. A movement was created.

I believe there are plenty of opportunities for everyone. There was enough for all. I am asking you to ACT! Advance your life. Create a wonderful life for yourself and others. Create your future. You have great power. Be the best version of yourself.

What will you do?

"Each time we face our fear, we gain strength, courage, and confidence in the doing"–Unknown.

Trust in your ability. Aim for the stars, my readers. Everyday, you have the choice to make it a day closer to your dreams or take a step backwards. I have faith as you check off your goals. Your desires will become truth. Your dreams will be a reality.

Fallen Redwood Tree
Leggett, California

CHAPTER 32

APRIL 11, 2016

I awoke to a crisp morning. It was so peaceful by the stream; I could hear the water from outside of the truck as I was curled up in the sleeping bag. I used the WiFi to post to Facebook. It was lovely catching up on emails and sharing updates on social media accounts. When I left my temporary home, I was hungry. Unfortunately, I did not feel like preparing any type of breakfast. I decided instead to stop at a café in the next town and enjoy a hot meal.

I attempted to start a fire. I planned to burn one piece of wood and save the other two for a future camping night. Sadly, everything I had to start a fire with was damp. The wood would not burn, only smoke. I saved the rest in hope it would dry out.

As I pulled out for the day's adventure, I noticed a true blessing. The sky was cloudless and a luminous blue. It even made the water seem clearer. The waves were breaking on the rocky shore creating a natural musical feast for my ears. I almost parked somewhere just to marvel in its beauty.

As I was leaving Westport, I noticed I had about a two-hour drive to Eureka, California. The road remained curvy, though I could drive a tad faster. I enjoyed driving slowly and savoring those precious moments. I rarely encountered a car behind me pressuring to go faster, which was pleasant. The road hugged the coast for about thirty minutes. Then, suddenly, it transitioned as if I were in a whole new world. I had moved away from the Pacific Ocean into a dense forest.

The views were only of trees: an impenetrable forest with a two-lane asphalt path. The road's architecture required a 20-mph speed limit. There were lots of those turn-outs, large and hidden. I considered using them in the future to spend the night.

I drove for about two hours, enjoying the roller coaster ride. I came across the occasional residential area. What caught me off guard was a logging truck driving those roads faster than I was. I also thought about how I would love to have a history lesson on the road itself, to see pictures of the land before the road was created. How had it been possible to build a road through rough terrain? Did they have to cut down trees, or carve through the mountainous hills? How was the layout of the road determined?

APRIL 11, 2016

As I made way further from the ocean, I noticed a road on the map which was closer to the ocean. Unfortunately, as I was driving, I never saw any type of road sign or exit for the coastal road. Highway 1 North brought me into Leggett, California. I detected an attraction, Drive-Thru Tree Park. I had to check it out. There was a redwood tree one could drive through, Chandelier Tree. There was also a gift shop and a picnic area.

As I approached the tree, it appeared large enough for the truck to easily fit through the opening. As I entered, the antenna bent over. I was afraid it might break. Then I scraped the passenger side mirror against the tree and left some scuff marks on it. I pulled the driver side mirror inward to protect it. Before heading into the tree I was using the phone to video the experience, but when the antenna bent I dropped the phone into my lap and ruined the video. I was going to either go back through it, ride my bike through it, or simply walk through again recording. But suddenly, a long line of cars began showing up. So, I simply made some lunch and walked around taking a few pictures of the redwoods. A gentleman from Michigan walked up to me and started a conversation. He was heading south with his family. We talked about my music and book. He explained how he wanted to ride the Pacific Coast Highway on a bicycle. We all had dreams!

Leaving Leggett, the plan was to stop in Eureka. I thought I would stay the night in a hotel to catch up on laundry and find a place to mountain bike. I had researched earlier in the day about performing somewhere. Sadly, I could not find any open mics or reliable information about performing on the streets.

Based on the road atlas I was using, I would be on the 101 freeway the entire way until I reached Eureka. But fortunately, there was still alluring scenery along the freeway. I flew through trees and past a divine river twisting along the path. I noticed a service road running alongside the river. Unfortunately, I could never locate a way to access it. When I reached Miranda, there was an exit to follow the Avenue of the Giants, found within the Humboldt Redwoods State Park. I assumed it would take me through the redwood forest. I had no hesitation. I exited onto the route. One could stop at a pull-off to take part in an auto tour. I noticed there were stopping points with informational signs along the route. I paused at one pull-off to snap some pictures and a video of the redwood trees. Of course, they were enormous, giants reaching way up into the sky. I realized later there were mountain bike trails. I wished I had known about them at the time. I could have seen those giants up close and personal, recording with the GoPro from the bike.

As I continued, the blue skies transformed to grey. At least the temperature was not too cold. I noticed several homeless people walking the streets there. The locals called them vagrants. During the tour, I noticed the homeless population in our country was immense.

APRIL 11, 2016

I believed most of the homeless people I saw needed psychological assistance.

I stopped in Eureka to design a strategy. I researched mountain bike trails as well as hotels. After figuring out the best direction, I chose to drive a little farther north to Arcata, California. I purchased a hotel room for the night. The next day, I planned on doing laundry and locating an area I could mountain bike. The gym I belonged to was nowhere to be found. I had gone more than 10 days without lifting. The hotel bed was the first bed I had slept in for about a week. I had stayed in a bed in Long Beach, but only for about four to five hours. I was truly grateful for seeing the brilliance surrounding me.

As I viewed the atlas, it showed I would be on the freeway at least to Coos Bay, Oregon. There were some sights I desired to see in Oregon. I wanted to ensure I did not miss them like I had the waterfall. The road atlas did not list any free camping in the area. Yet there were lots of camping opportunities through campgrounds. Whether or not I camped depended on their prices. As I drove, I noticed many roadside attractions to stop and visit.

I laid in bed, stretching out, and realized I needed to review some lessons learned from my readings: *I am good enough. Maintain confidence in your abilities. I could achieve anything and everything. Simply do your best on each task each day. Let God worry about the outcomes. Locate a street and perform. Be on stage in front of strangers. Continue to have unwavering faith. My responsibilities are to plan, to utilize my skills, to share my creativity. Then, turn it over to the public. Do not stress or worry if they clap or boo or decide not to purchase music.*

Secret Camping Site
Oregon

CHAPTER 33

APRIL 12, 2016

I attempted to sleep in. I remained under the covers to enjoy the bed of the hotel. I believed I awoke first at 6:00 a.m. I then drifted back into a dream world. Then around 8:30 a.m., I awoke again. I stayed in bed and watched TV. I updated my social media accounts before preparing for the day. The hotel check-out was 11:00 a.m.; I left the room around 11:15 a.m.

Before heading out of town, I decided I should do laundry and fuel the truck. I located a laundromat to wash and dry my clothes, got some lunch, and after purchasing gas, I jumped on the North Highway 101 freeway. Per the map, most of the trip would be on the freeway at 65 mph instead of the snake-like roads I had driven earlier. The destination was Brookings, Oregon. There was a state park there with bicycle trails, only costing $20 a night.

The atmosphere changed. As far as I could see, the people in the area were different than those I had encountered in Southern California or in my more familiar environs in Florida and Mississippi. No longer the tanned, athletic, toned bodies. Instead, I saw a lot of flannel and hiking boots. The stereotypical grunge appearance seemed to be quite popular.

I was pleasantly surprised as I drove. Most of the day was spent along the freeway. At moments, the road transitioned back into the curvy, winding lanes more fun to drive. I was in a constant anticipation to see what would be around the next curve.

Along the trek, I noticed an exit returning through a redwood forest. I jumped at the opportunity and reduced speed to about 35 mph and rode through the land of the giants again. There were multiple trailheads along the route. I thought about stopping to take a walk or seeing if I could ride my mountain bike. Instead, I chose to continue driving north. I always sensed a clock ticking in the back of my mind. I had to move forward. I had a deadline.

Though it was not on the road atlas, I approached an area to stop and view wild elk. It was a small gravel lot between two green fields. I stopped for about 20 minutes, hoping to see an elk. No luck. As I drove up the road a short way, there were cabins for rent. Behold, in the field next to the cabins was a herd of female elk. They were sitting around. They almost appeared tame. People were walking within about 50 yards of them. The elk did not respond or try to move. It was as if they were used to the presence of humans.

I continued driving, though I began to feel very tired. I thought about stopping in Crescent City, California. It was about 45-minutes short of the planned destination. Supposedly, there was possible free camping sites available. To locate them, I would have to turn onto a new road to drive an uncertain distance. I paused to inquire about the local hotel rates. However, a little voice inside told me to keep moving forward. So, I put the truck in drive and completed the last 45-minutes to the original destination.

I arrived in Brookings; it was a considerably larger town than most I had driven through on the trip located on Highway 1/101. I possessed limited cash in hand. I was on the lookout for a bank, preferably my personal bank to reduce possible fees. I drove to the Harris Beach State Park, for possible camping overnight. It was $20, to be paid in cash. There was not an attendant. It was situated on the Pacific Ocean, except the camping spots were not. I rode through the camping area. It was okay. The small spots offered some privacy including a picnic table and a fire ring. I could ride my bike into town or around the campground. Sadly, there were no true mountain bike trails. Instead, I headed back into town. On the highway of an unknown name was another state park offering camping for only $22 a night. There was also some other possibly free camping further up the road from the state park.

As I arrived at the Alfred A. Loeb State Park, my first impression was how far off the highway it was located, almost eight miles. I drove through the campground. It was swell. It provided multiple spots offering privacy, a picnic table and a fire ring. The difference was the park was above a river. One could walk down to fish or trek along the shore. Once again though, the park had no attendant. I needed cash to pay.

Instead of returning to town, I went on a new adventure to discover the free camping listed on the map. I advanced, driving the two-lane road into the forest. I came to a sign signifying the area as a wildlife preserve. The road narrowed as I was leaving the County Road. It continued winding until I finally saw pull-off areas. I then came to a sign with boating information. About four miles into the new adventure, I noticed several boat ramp access points down to the river. I drove by the first one accidentally. But when I reached the second one, I entered to see what was down there. I found a restroom and a rough entry boat ramp. I noticed someone was camping out, as their fire was burning. It dawned on me I could camp at a site for free. I left to locate another place. I progressed to another location where I almost stayed. I parked on the river bank. The bathrooms were up the hill. I knew it might rain during the night, which would make it difficult to leave the campsite since the truck was not equipped with four-wheel drive. The incline was steep. I struggled exiting some, even on the dry dirt. I drove and drove for what felt like another 30 minutes up into the mountains. I finally turned around and told myself I would figure out a new plan or stop at the very first boat ramp to see if it were empty. I turned the truck around in a small residential area where a gentleman was outside working on his car. I stopped and asked about camping in the area and where the road eventually ended. He told me the road continued going up into the woods after it crossed a one-lane bridge. He mentioned there was a pull-off to the right up a hill or a pull-off to the left descending down by the river. He was confident my truck could do either, even if it did rain. I thanked him and turned the truck back in the original direction. I neared the one-lane bridge and crossed it to see what was ahead. The road ended at an intersection where one had to choose left or right. Both directions were dirt and gravel roads. The signs designated some landmarks about 18 miles away. Instead, I turned around and choose to drive down by the river. When I arrived, I was about a quarter-mile off the road. I saw remnants of old campsite fire pits where people had stacked rocks to contain the flames. The drive in was a little rough and had areas where people had put their trucks into four-wheel drive and had some fun in the mud. I parked on the plateau of the hill, which was all gravel instead of going all the way down to the beach area like most people did. I walked down to the beach area. There were remnants from the people who had been there before. There were two large fire pits with a lot of trash around. Across the river was a green grassland area, where cows were grazing. The river water was quite clear and fast moving. Several branches of other streams flowed into it. I created a new fire ring on the gravel plateau near the truck. I gathered firewood. I decided it was the place to stay. I saw the occasional car heading in the direction of the one-lane bridge, but no one came into the area where I was. The wood was very dry and ignited quickly. Using only one paper towel as starting fuel, the fire was soon blazing. I prepared dinner and caught up on reading for about two good hours before the rain began. I sat in the truck watching the fire smoke as the rain dampened it, as well as the remainder of firewood I had gathered. If I wanted to remain dry, I was stuck in the truck for the rest of the night. I remembered the weather report had predicted rain for the next couple of days. With the rain only a drizzle, I retrieved binoculars from the storage trunk in the back of the truck bed. Perhaps in the morning something besides cows would be grazing in the meadow. I planned to reach Coos Bay, Oregon, the next day. I would check out the possibility of an open mic or street performance, though weather in this particular area of the country reduced the opportunities to perform on the street due to the colder temperatures and the omnipresent threat of rain.

I was truly blessed and grateful. I was camping in an amazing, free location in Oregon. It was along a river with mountains in the distance, cows grazing across the river, and I had been able to build a great warm fire. The rain did come, but it would be music as I fell asleep.

I continued to remain positive. Live with love, creativity and imagination. I was happy. I was successful. I was a light. I desired to illuminate brightly. I desired to be seen from the darkest sky.

I imagined myself covered in body armor. I was protected. I had inner strength. I believed in myself. I continued to improve myself daily. I thought, "The more I work on myself, the less time I have to criticize or compare myself to others."

We all come from different backgrounds. Many others had unimaginable odds against them. But, if you look closely, someone worse off had attracted success. I was willing to be homeless chasing my dreams rather than working a day job I hated going to. I chose to find a way through the darkness to the light.

Bring your dreams into reality. Feel it in your bones. Make the choice to overcome your fears. Take the leap of faith. Baby steps worked very well. Or, simply jump like I did from an airplane. Choose to see the things which do not exist. Pay attention to your heart and instincts. Trust me, they will steer you right. I believe you have greatness within you. Say to yourself: "The world belongs to me."

Make the choice to change your life. You are only here a short time. We never know our last breath. Do not waste it. If you fail, get up and keep working on yourself.

Oregon Coast Line
Highway 1

CHAPTER 34

APRIL 13, 2016

I awoke in the morning with a spirit of love and gratitude. It was an incredible feeling. I didn't want to stay too long at the camp site; I was parked on dirt, and if I attempted to take a hike I would just create a muddy mess. I tried to see wildlife with the binoculars. Unfortunately, only the cows were present, so I chose to leave the beauty and drive down the road a few miles to a bathroom. I took a sponge bath on the concrete floor then put on fresh clean clothes.

The drive varied from the freeway, where I could travel 65 mph, to serpent curves with a speed limit of 25 mph. At times, I was riding next to the Pacific Ocean. Then within minutes I found myself driving through the forest by an alluring river. At one point, I drove past the Oregon Dunes National Recreation Area. It was a park featuring huge coastal mounds of sand as tall as 500 feet hiding the Pacific Ocean from the road. I noticed many of those state parks provided access to the sand dunes. The place was a dream for people who owned motorcycles, ATVs, or Razors. I also saw a few places where one could rent recreational vehicles to ride.

I thought about staying the night at a state park for $20, but I had noticed some possible free camping sites along the way. I wanted to check them out first. I searched but unfortunately, I could not find any. I continued driving north passing town after town and state park after state park. The terrain continued to transition from the Pacific Ocean with the water smashing against the rocks and waves rolling in onto the beaches. Then, I went into the forest again, watching a winding river cut through the mountains.

I stopped briefly a few times to ensure I did not miss any significant sights along the way. One spot I wanted to see, Crater Lake, was located inland, almost four hours away from the coast. So, I moved forward.

When I arrived in Coos Bay, it resembled a fishing town straight out of a vintage magazine. I craved some fish and chips for lunch. Feeling quite tired, I stopped at a local seafood restaurant. As I sat at the table, I wondered where I would be staying for the night. After the tasty lunch, I located a bicycle shop to ask about mountain bike trails and free camping. She gave me a map of possible bike trails. Regrettably, they were about a half hour inland. The road atlas showed a possible free camping site. After driving for about 20 minutes, I could not find it.

As I departed Coos Bay, I saw a site called Thor's Well was within 30 minutes. Thor's Well released jets of water. They were pumped into the air by the power of the ocean tide and waves. As I approached the area, it began to rain. I was thinking I would get a hotel room instead of camping out. It was difficult to camp in the truck when it rained. It created a mess. I was stuck in the front seat trying to read, write, and catch up. Besides, I couldn't make a fire.

I had seen a free campsite on the internet earlier. Unfortunately, my phone had no service. I was not able to access the GPS maps to find it. There were a few roads offering turn offs. I had had some good fortune with those types of roads, locating camping sites with some privacy. The roads were dirt service roads which I wanted to avoid due to the rain. Instead, I continued driving until I found the hotel I had seen online earlier. It was located on the ocean and cost less than $100 per night.

With the rain and wind voiding my vision, I realized I had missed Thor's Well as I was driving towards the hotel. The winds increased violently. I watched the ocean crash against the shoreline. Mother Nature could be quite powerful.

The next day, with weather permitting, I planned to head south again to find Thor's Well and do some hiking before making my way further north. I had been driving around 100 to 150 miles per day. I had faith I would continue to find free, awe-inspiring, safe campsites in the future.

Once checked into the hotel, I glanced into the mirror. I noticed I was developing a sty in my right eye. I thought I had some medicine in the truck.

Even though I had stayed in a hotel room just the other night, I felt quite sluggish. *I loved what I was undertaking. I was following my bliss. Unfortunately, I was drained. I was enjoying the traveling and writing much more than the performing. While performing was fun and enjoyable, I was becoming more comfortable as an author. I was excited for the many future Country Boy travel adventures to follow.*

The weather worsened outside. I could hear the rain pounding against the glass. The high winds created sheets of downpour. *I thought there were storms in our lives. I had faith I was strong enough to come through them and to carry on. I was filled with peace and harmony. I maintained faith the circumstance would change.*

Today was yours. You can break through as well. Continue with your positive attitude. You are a hero. Believe in yourself - whatever storms you might be in shall pass. You will see sunny days.

"*Our world, our life is a place of mystery, light, and magic; simply open your eyes.*" – Dan Millman

What battles have you had? "*He knows he has learned something with every battle he has fought. But many of those lessons have caused him unnecessary suffering. More than*

APRIL 13, 2016

once he has wasted his time fighting for a lie. And he has suffered for people who did not deserve his love. Only risk your heart for something worthwhile" – Paulo Coelho.

We all have battles we face, though most of the time, the battle is with ourselves. We desired a higher self of consciousness. Yet we continue our self-negative self-talk to ourselves.

Times might get tough. If it were with someone else, we could simply walk away. But with one's own self, we see ourselves in the mirror every day. Begin with positive thoughts. You can defeat the evil voice inside. Through time, your inner voice becomes your biggest cheerleader. YOU CAN!

Passing of The Storm
By Tommy Ray

Don't be shy, don't be afraid
The storm will pass to sunny days

I am sitting alone watching storms outside
Listening to the thunder like a lull-a-by
The lighting strikes and blinds my eyes
As the rain pours and the wind blows by

I close my eyes asking for better days
Hoping those dreams of mind don't die away
My soul cries wondering how far are they
Until I hear a voice inside saying today was the day

Don't be shy, don't be afraid
The storm shall pass to sunny days
Open your eyes to better times

I look to the mirror and wipe away the rain
Wondering where to find my dreams
Having faith, the storm will pass
So, don't be shy and don't be afraid

Sunset Over the Pacific Ocean
Oregon Coastline

CHAPTER 35
APRIL 14, 2016

I awoke in the hotel bed at 6:30 a.m. Why was I awake so early? The room was toasty. The curtains were drawn close. The bed was comfortable. It was about the same time I awakened when sleeping in the back seat of the truck. The only difference was I did not wake up in the middle of the night cold or trying to find a new and more comfortable position. I laid in bed, attempting to fall back to sleep. I used a visualization technique pertaining to my goals. The weird thing was my mind drifted back to 1991. Images of a pep rally for the basketball team, with me speaking to the student body, appeared. My mind worked in odd ways. It was still raining outside. The room was on the parking lot side so I could not see Mother Nature at her best. I decided it was wise to have a hot breakfast. When I entered the restaurant, I sat by the windows closest to the ocean. I was in awe of her strength.

The waitress mentioned to the people at another table next to me it was the worst storm they had seen so late in the year in almost a decade. The rain was falling sideways as the ocean waves battered the rocks and shoreline. It was an astonishing show. I thought, would anyone be crazy enough to surf those conditions?

I sat alone. They had placed me at a table for four. The young lady server approached. She began to remove the other place settings. I asked her to please wait…"I have three invisible friends joining me." She smiled and laughed. She removed the other cups and silverware. I asked why, and she replied, "It's because of health reasons and the potential for unsanitary conditions." I laughed, as it seemed she was calling me dirty and unclean. Anyway, she smiled and chuckled, which was always a positive thing when a man talked to a woman. When she brought me the orange juice bare-handed, I asked if she had washed her hands first. Once again, she blushed and grinned. About five minutes later, she was setting the table next to me and ensuring the napkins and silverware were placed correctly. I told her I thought it would be a horrible job for an OCD waitress. Once again, she laughed out loud.

As time passed over the next hour or so, the weather around the hotel began to clear and the rain stopped. I thought it would be a great opportunity to check out and head back south to find Thor's Well. I asked for directions at the hotel. I thought I had known where it was. It was only about five minutes south. The rain was pouring a few miles south of the hotel, causing the road visibility to be greatly reduced. Once again, I was amazed the cars approaching me did not have their headlights on. I drove south for 10 more minutes. I turned around and parked where I thought I was supposed to park to view the well. Unfortunately, with the wind and rain, I was not able to attempt the hike or see anything. About two miles north was a park for Devil's Churn. I stopped and spoke with the woman about Thor's Well. She told me I was in the correct spot but had to walk a trail and then climb and go out on some rocks to see it. She advised me in those conditions, it was not a safe thing to do. I decided it was best to head north instead of waiting to see if the weather cleared. It could be another four to five hours.

I continued north on Highway 1. I was surprised how tired I remained. Normally, after a night in a hotel, I was refreshed. Perhaps I needed multiple nights in a hotel bed. In addition, I had not worked out in over a week. My body was also probably angry with the unclean food I had been putting into my system.

The first sizable town I came to was Newport. It was quite lovely and had a Wal-Mart. I stopped to purchased supplies and contemplated taking a nap or even just staying the night. I had only driven about an hour. With the assistance of WiFi, I learned my gym was only about 30 minutes north of me in Lincoln City. It would be a place for me to sleep before heading to Portland the next day.

As I drove north. the highway changed as it had been doing all along during this leg of the trip. One minute I had the Pacific Ocean to the left and was watching the waves crash against the boulders. Then, I would be in a forest with a winding stream to my right. No matter what the scenery offered, it was stunning.

About 10 minutes before I arrived in Lincoln City, I stopped and ate lunch at a BBQ place. Once inside, I learned the owner competed in BBQ competitions. The walls displayed prize ribbons. As I placed my order, we spoke about my tour and my music. I asked if he would like to donate and receive an autographed EP.

I ordered the smoked pulled chicken with the owner's grandfather's sauce and his competition sauce. My sides were traditional baked beans and greens. They would have made my Granny Ray in Mississippi jealous. Normally, cornbread was treated as a vegetable when ordering, but he gave it to me for free. The food was divine. After I finished the meal, we talked some more. He donated $20 for an EP of *Crossroads*. The restaurant also had a program which allowed customers to buy a meal at cost. The owner then donated the meal to someone who could not afford it. He considered the program a way to "pay it forward." I thought it was a keen idea. The owner also told me about some places I could stop in Lincoln City to ask if I could perform. Overall, the visit at the BBQ restaurant was a fantastic experience, a true blessing.

APRIL 14, 2016

As I entered Lincoln City, the first bar was right in the beginning of town, so I stopped. I went inside around 3:00 p.m. There was already a crowd of about six to eight people drinking. I overheard one guy on the phone saying he was in a meeting and would be available in about an hour. From a music standpoint, they were booked or else having karaoke over the next few days. As I was walking out, a gentleman stopped me and began asking me questions about myself and my trip. I spoke with him briefly. He was probably harmless. Yet, something felt odd. I departed before hitting him up for a donation or sharing too much personal information about myself.

Next door to the bar was a marijuana dispensary. Being from the East Coast, I had never seen one. I was curious. I went inside. I had to first show my ID at a window. Then a person behind a locked door buzzed me into another room through the locked door. They handed me a menu and asked if I wanted to buy anything. I told them not to laugh…I was on tour and passing through. I had never seen a marijuana dispensary and desired to see what it was all about. The girl helping me was from outside of Philly. She spoke to me about the different types of marijuana they sold, pre-rolled, or loose. Certain types were designed to help one zone out, perhaps sleep; those gave the smoker the munchies. Some were meant to enhance one's creativity. The high potency choices were $12 a gram. I had no clue how much a gram was. She had me smell different varieties to take in their aroma. I asked how to smoke it. She said to either break it up and put it into a pipe. Or buy some papers to put it in to roll and smoke like a cigarette. I was tempted yet chose not to purchase any marijuana. The laws varied from state to state. I could freely buy marijuana in one state legally and then get busted and arrested in another for the legally purchased marijuana. I didn't want to risk it. Later in my trip, I thought, I would try marijuana at least once. I had not smoked pot since I was an undergrad in 1992. I did not even know if I had smoked it right because I was using a friend's bong.

I located the gym as I drove into the town further. The town itself was quite grand. I contemplated obtaining another motel room or at least taking a nap in the parking lot. I walked inside the gym. It was splendid and offered a shower. I really had no desire to work out. I only wanted to sleep.

After a brief workout, I enjoyed a hot shower. I returned to the truck in the parking lot. I had two options: either return to the state park and pay $21 to camp overnight; or drive about 20 minutes north to explore some free camping possibilities. I weighed the options and drove north.

Once outside of the town, I was in the middle of nowhere again. It happened so quickly outside of those coastal towns. I went from having phone service to no signal within a mile or less. Once I departed a town and drove about five minutes around those curvy roads, I had no desire to turn around. I only wanted to keep moving forward. I likened it to my dreams. I sensed around each curve my dreams were going to come true. So, I continued driving and driving. And of course, it helped when the scenery was gorgeous.

I approached the turnoff which the map indicated led to the free campsite. It resembled Deliverance country. The most interesting thing about the highway was the fast-moving stream flowing next to the road. I was hoping to find a camping spot like the one I'd found the other night next to the stream. I allowed 10 miles to locate a spot before turning around. I passed two campgrounds and a few turnoff roads, perhaps leading to some secluded free camping. I reached the ten-mile boundary and turned around. I stopped at the first campground. It was free, in a field containing only a few other tents. They were set up with no cars in the parking lot. It seemed like not a good place for me. I chose one of the roads I had seen previously. I began driving up it. It was leading me further up into the mountains. I really saw no place to stop to camp and wished again I had a four-wheel drive truck. When I finally came to a place to turn around, I did, and headed back down to the main road. I told myself I would give it one last try at the other campground. It had a sign for horseback riding. I was told earlier, any time I saw those type of trails, they were also good for mountain biking. When I turned toward the campground, it had a number '14' on the sign post. I was hoping it did not mean it was 14 miles up the road. I drove about seven miles and thought, "Yep, exactly what the sign meant." So, I decided to turn around and return to Highway 1 to find a state park. I noticed most of the state parks in Oregon charged $21 a night for a tent. If one was a hiker or bike rider, it was only $6. After a few more miles of driving by ranches and streams, the Pacific Ocean popped its magnificent head out again. Unfortunately, the campground did not offer views of the ocean. Though, it was splendid in its own right. There were lots of spaces available. The campground offered bathrooms and showers. I located a spot in the back for some privacy. I was happy because even far away from the water, I could still hear the thunderous sounds from the waves crashing against the sandy beaches.

After I returned from paying, I noticed an odd thing. Someone had set up their camp site right next to me. I did not understand why. With over a hundred empty spots and a lot of those with privacy, the father and son chose to set up next to me. Sometimes, I just could not understand how other people thought. As I wrote in my journal along with writing this book, I had to listen to their voices, their sneezes and coughing. At least the soothing power of the ocean's ceaseless waves were also in my ear.

As darkness approached, I sat there listening to my fire crackling, the sounds of the ocean pounding, as well as the rustling of the father and son in the background.

APRIL 14, 2016

It made me ask, "What did I do today to cause this intrusion?" I could have understood their choice if the campground had been full, but it was almost completely empty. You might ask, why did I not relocate? I already had everything out and the fire ring prepared or else I would have. When one paid, one also had to mark the spot on the payment envelope. So, once I had picked a spot, it was mine. Perhaps the people overlooking the campground would have understood if I would have asked permission to change locations.

I could remain at the campsite until 1:00 p.m. the following day. I doubted they would have known if I had stayed longer. The plan of the next day's drive would probably have me reach Portland. I had a friend, Matt, who attended Physician Assistant school with me in Savannah, Georgia. He would be in Portland on Monday visiting friends. If I stayed to say hello to him, it meant at least three nights in Portland. With it being such a large city, I was sure they had a Wal-Mart and the gym as well. I also planned to check out the music scene to perform.

It was the first night in a while with clear skies. The moon and stars were out. I wanted to enjoy them. The ocean was harmonious. As I sat in my red camping chair, I was mesmerized by the colorful flames. From the darkness I heard a rustling noise behind me in the bushes. I turned around quickly and shone a flashlight. I was startled by a large raccoon. It probably weighed close to 30 pounds. I tried to keep an eye on it to ensure it did not get too close to me. It approached. It was only six feet away. I left the camping chair on the ground and sat on top of the picnic table by the fire. I did not desire to turn in yet or be forced to hide in the truck by a raccoon. I had to make a noise to scare it off when it was less than two feet away from me.

I now knew why I had to be careful leaving food out in particular parts of the country. No telling what would come out to obtain it. Tonight, it was a raccoon; the next it could be a bear. Right after scaring it off, I turned around and the raccoon was only a foot behind me.

It was absurd how easy it was to get my heart pounding and pulse pumping out in the wilderness, being surprised by a live animal. Next, I heard frogs croaking. The woods lit up with activity at night. Maybe it was why they seemed so scary to me.

As night wore on, a rainstorm passed through the area. I noticed frequent storms were a common occurrence in the region. I was blessed before I went to bed, I could gaze upon the moon and stars for a short while. The people next to me were quiet, at least for now. The moment in time was tranquil.

Camping Spot Wildlife
Oregon

CHAPTER 36
APRIL 15, 2016

During the night, I became chilled, primarily the parts of me uncovered by the sleeping bag. I had added an extra layering of clothing before climbing into the sleeping bag the previous night. I tossed and turned, attempting to find a comfortable position. There were only three in the truck's back seat: I could lay on my back with my knees bent or curled up like a baby either on my right or left side.

When I awoke, the sun was trying hard to break through the clouds. I lit a fire. Then the peaceful morning changed to coughing, sneezing, and throat clearing from the people next to me. I was excited because it seemed they were packing up. Sadly, they were only moving their things into the sunshine to dry out. They talked about dog poop and turned on a radio.

I walked to the shower house in the campground. It was not too bad. The water remained on for about 3 minutes. You had to hit a silver button to maintain the flow. At least it was part of the overnight fee instead of by quarters. The positive: the water remained hot the entire time.

I decided to consume a small breakfast. As I did, I watched a few birds playing around me. I looked over my map and decided I wanted to camp out one more night before driving on to Portland. My friend Matt from Pittsburgh didn't arrive until Monday. I thought if I spent a second night there, I would only have to stay two nights in Portland rather than three. I talked myself into moving forward. There was a countdown clock in my head. I had to return to Mississippi for the Awards Show. I wanted to visit many more cities to share the Tommy Ray Music brand.

I departed the campground and churned my way up the highway. I decided to stop and purchase some marijuana if I came across another dispensary. Since it was legal, I thought I might as well try it. I planned on buying some to enhance my creativity and help me sleep better.

The first nice-sized town I entered was Tillamook. Since I knew I was going to camp tonight, I needed something to grill over a fire pit. I stopped at a Safeway grocery store for supplies. Inside, it resembled a Publix I had used in Florida. It had a delectable deli. In addition, it had everything one could ask for from a food standpoint.

APRIL 15, 2016

It also had free WiFi inside. As I pushed the shopping cart through the store, I caught up on my e-mail and social media. I purchased bacon and hamburger meat. I also stocked up on fruit. I was not eating many vegetables on the tour either. I was trying to consume three different types of fruit a day to compensate.

I exited the store. From a distance, I saw a mother and child on the corner asking for help. It made me feel sad. I did see a few people dropping off bags of items and some offered her money. I wondered how long she had been there. It was Friday. Her daughter looked old enough to have been in school.

About 30 minutes up the road I entered a town called Rockaway Beach. It had a marijuana dispensary on the main highway. I parked and ventured inside. I told the gentleman it was my first time inside a dispensary. He offered me a menu and talked about the different strengths and purposes of the various varieties of marijuana they sold. He offered me the plant either in a bud or already in a joint. If I took the bud. I would have to buy a pipe. Instead, I purchased two pre-made joints. I bought one Passion-Lavender-Haze for creativity and one Blue Grape to help me sleep. The Passion one was $9.00, and the Blue was $11. As I made my purchase, I wondered how many puffs I would have to take before I might feel something. I was hoping only a few would create the relaxation and creative state I desired. With only a few tokes, I could use each joint multiple times. It only took one beer to provide a buzz for me. Since it was the first time I had smoked pot since 1992, I was thinking the same thing would happen with the joints as happened with the beer.

I located two state parks on the map. One cost $29, and the other $11. I went to the $29 one first. It offered the basic amenities of a space, picnic table, and fire pit. The private spots were taken. I decided to move on to the second park. It took me about an hour to reach the other park. I had to take a side road about 20 miles. The campground was up a winding road, another seven miles. When I reached the top, the campground was a parking lot where you hiked yourself in to find a designated site. Since I did not have a tent, I thought it was pointless to sleep in an open parking lot for $11 with no privacy. Instead, I jumped back into the silver horse and returned to the original campground. In hindsight, I should have just stayed. The campground contained paths to ride bikes on.

The sites to park were located behind sand dunes. I could not see the ocean, but I could hear it. The spots were not very private. They were primarily geared for RV campers. I drove around the campground to locate the best spot offering privacy. I wanted to be as far away from campers as possible. I picked a spot where no one was around me on either side. As evening approached, more people arrived at the campground. Someone pulled in about three spots over. Unfortunately, in the campground, one could see everything all around. I put up a grey tarp between two trees on the right side. It provided some privacy from the RV on the right.

I unpacked and set up the camp. The campsite included my camping chair, the backseat bed, along with a pile of sticks and wood for the fire. Afterwards, I went for a bike ride on those surrounding trails. The campsite offered a two-mile paved trail you could ride or walk on. They also had a few horse trails I wanted to check out. The campsite offered a section for horses. People could bring their horses - each site had a stable - and ride along the wooded trails and the beach. The first paved path was like the path back home in Mississippi around the reservoir. It was predominantly flat and smooth. There was also an airstrip on the campground which I thought was pretty neat. Near the airstrip, the campground opened to a bay along with a swell beach area. The beach was divine. It had remnants of old trees and driftwood scattered around. The water in the bay was low, but I thought it was probably low tide.

On the way back to my camping spot, riding around a curve, I almost collided with two deer. They must have been used to people. They did not run and continued eating grass as I approached. I watched them for about five minutes. I was only about three feet away from them. They would look up, then put their heads back down to eat. They were slowly grazing their way toward my campsite. As I pushed on towards it, I saw another deer grazing. The campground's website mentioned campers might see deer and some elk. I would be careful about dropping food around the campsite. I did not want any uninvited wild guests. During the bike ride, I noticed signs warning campers to watch out for cougars. I had never seen a cougar in the wild. I did not want to as they seemed aggressive.

I ignited the fire pit. Unfortunately, it was mostly white smoke. The wood I purchased must have been damp. I was able to have some colorful flames. As I sat in the red camping chair, my curiosity finally got the best of me. I took out the Passion-Lavender-Haze joint, lit the end, and puffed a few times. I probably smoked about a quarter of it, about five to six good hits, but did not feel anything. I did not want to push it by inhaling too much at one time. I know with alcohol, I often have a delayed effect. I can drink a beer but not feel the intoxicating effects until an hour or so later. Since I was not feeling anything from the puffs I had taken, I thought I better wait to see if the marijuana gave me the same delayed effect as alcohol. I waited for about two hours and can officially say those tokes did not do anything to me or for me.

The sky was clear, but cold. The frogs croaked in the background. I thought perhaps I might see some stars come out before I retired to bed. With no fire, it was not fun sitting outside in the dark all alone. I had never bought a lantern for the tour.

There were more campers entering the park after dark. I was losing the small amount of privacy I had. I had hoped to camp out more during the tour. However, things didn't seem to be working out as I planned. I was hoping to locate more free campsites with privacy, but also amazing views. The camp by the river was in my top five so far, at least before it began to rain.

I decided to attempt one more time to ignite a fire. I thought I might stay there until noon the next day to ride my bike on those horse trails. I was in no hurry to arrive in Portland. It was an easy two-hour drive. If I stayed there a little longer, it wouldn't mess up my plans. I planned to stay in a hotel room for two nights.

Every campsite there offered water and electric hookups which was one reason it cost more. They had security lights at each site offering some light. It was almost 9:00 p.m. People were still out walking or riding their bikes. I threw an empty squeeze bottle of mayo into the fire over the hot coals. The flame intensified. I wondered what was in mayo to make it generate a flame?

I could hear the ocean in the distant background. It would be a little sad leaving it for a few days as I headed into Portland. Speaking of sad things, when I was driving through some of those backroads, I noticed they were clear-cutting timber. After the beauty of the forests I had seen on the tour, seeing the once-green land stripped of its trees was quite depressing. I was sure we needed the lumber. But, what a drastic change cutting down all those trees caused in the overall landscape. I also wondered how they could cut down trees on some of those steep hillsides.

I relocated into the truck. With the sleeping bag wrapped around my body along with my head propped on the pillow, I pondered the future.

I was asking millions of people to find value in my products. Those included the music I composed as well as the books I authored. I was asking people to spend their money on me. I was pushing myself to create inspiration to others. I desired to move them, make their heart beat faster, make them think.

I was responsible for myself. I told myself it was my fault if I do not sell a million copies of books, EP's, or blogs on Tommy Ray Insights. It was my fault if I did not visit Portugal or learn to surf in Costa Rica due to fear. I could not blame anyone else if I did not reach my dreams. It was because I failed to work hard enough, market correctly, or improve my skills. It was all on me!

I continued my motto, "Dream big, anything was possible, live life like you cannot fail."

As I closed my eyes, one last thought crossed my mind. *I said thank you to Dr. Seuss: "Oh the Places You'll Go, congratulations! Today was your day. You're off to great places! You're off and away."*

The Coastline of Oregon

CHAPTER 37
APRIL 16, 2016

I awoke at 7:30 a.m. It was about an hour longer than I normally slept. It had also become hot in the truck. There was no breeze, so I had to remove my top layers and my shirt. I don't know if the marijuana had helped me sleep a little longer or if it had made me shrink in size like *Alice in Wonderland,* but I was able to stretch out more and be more comfortable. I exited the truck to move around. I planned to cook bacon and eggs for breakfast. Though warm inside the truck last night, it was still quite cold outside. I had to put on a jacket, headband, and gloves. I attempted to light the campfire again. Unfortunately, it only produced white smoke.

After preparing breakfast on the Butane stove, I went out on my bike. I found the horse trails to ride on. I rode onto one but noticed quickly the idea wasn't going to work. The trail consisted of loose deep sand to protect the horses' hooves. It was filled with horse droppings as well. As soon as I could find pavement, I rode my bike onto it. The pavement brought me to a boat ramp with some stunning views of the bay. I noticed a sign announcing a two-mile hard packed sand trail. It ended at a jetty.

The jetty was truly excellent. I leaned the bike against a tree, then walked about a quarter of mile out onto the jetty. The path of the water forced the waves to enter at about a two-foot tall peak. They then crashed into the jetty's sides. The walking trail was over loose rocks. There were moments where I had to climb over fallen trees to access the outer parts. I was able to near the entry to the Pacific Ocean. As I walked out, I observed something in the water. At first glance, I thought it was a diver looking for something. When I got closer, I saw three more figures. It turned out they were seals looking for food or playing. I watched them play for about 30 minutes. I also needed time to rest. Those two-miles on my bike had made me tired. The sun was high in the sky. The warmth it produced was enough to take off my shirt to catch some rays.

On my return to the campsite, I used an easier spinning gear. I could get back without stopping to rest. The trail itself was pleasing. It offered lots of wildflowers along with the occasional bird flying by. A few horses were entering the trail on my way out.

Back at the camp, I ate lunch and grabbed a shower. After a refreshing, long, hot shower, I figured out the day's plan. I had two ideas about what to do. The first was to drive up to Seaside, about 30 minutes north. I could see the town, fuel up the truck, and locate somewhere to update social media and check messages. Or, I could simply drive straight through to Portland.

I decided on the Seaside choice. When I arrived in Seaside, I noticed it was an attractive vintage town with a unique downtown area. There seemed to be a lot of options, especially for a Saturday night. I considered staying the night in a hotel. I was taken aback when I checked the rates. Even a basic Holiday Inn was $200 a night. I was sure the motels were a lot cheaper. However, in most of those I did not feel safe. I looked over the map. I saw I could go north toward Astoria and stay at a state park there for $21. I would have about a two-hour drive to Portland. Portland was only about an hour away from Seaside.

I noticed a state park in Buxton on Highway 26. It was the route I was going to take to Portland anyway. The problem was it only had hike-in camping, according to the website. The highway was taking me through a state forest. I would have the possibility of free camping if I chose to venture up into the mountains on an unmarked side road.

I decided to stop at the "Stub" Stewart State Park to see what they had to offer. When I arrived, it seemed like a paradise for mountain biking. There were over 25 miles of trails featuring all difficulty levels. The problem was the camping. Unless one had a horse, there were only two sections where one could camp. The pull-in spots were $31 a night, but there was no privacy. I spoke with a ranger who mentioned two other locations inside the park. When he found out I would be sleeping in the truck, he said there was only one option.

I drove to the site. Unfortunately, it was only an open field. The individual spots each had a picnic table, a fire ring, and room for a tent. There was no privacy. The campground was awesome. A top state park if one had a camper or a tent. Next trip, I intended to pack a tent. I could have purchased a spot for $21 to enjoy the picnic table and fire ring, but there would be no privacy sleeping in the truck as there would be cars parked right next to me on either side with campers behind me. Instead, I left. I drove into the state forest hoping to find a free camping site.

I gave myself 10 miles to find a turnoff road and turned left onto the first road I came to in the state forest. It was a winding gravel road up into the mountains. I drove along for three miles. No luck. Most of the area was used by logging trucks to remove timber. I met a truck coming the opposite way. I stopped and asked the driver about free camping in the area. He told me to keep going because there were little roads ahead branching off the main road. Some of those little roads were dead ends. He said people would camp there.

I continued up into the mountainous area for about two more miles before deciding to stop. As I was turning around, I noticed a van up the street appearing to be camping. I headed back down. On the way, I saw a turnoff I wanted to try, but a pick-up truck was already parked there so I kept going. A little way down, I heard a gunshot. I was glad I decided to leave. I believed it was some type of hunting season. It wouldn't have been safe for me out there with people shooting at wild game.

Once I returned to the main road, I said, "Portland, here I come." About 15 to 20 minutes outside the city, the drive maneuvered away from the coast. The drive transitioned into the hills and through farmland. Almost the entire way a stream ran parallel to the highway. I also noticed a temperature change. The forecast predicted temperatures in the 80s for the next two days in Portland, compared to the high 50s which I had been enjoying on the coast.

I pulled into Portland, which was the largest city in Oregon. Two major rivers connected into the city, the Willamette and Columbia. People first lived in the area in the 1830s. A positive aspect which I enjoyed: it was frequently recognized as one of the world's most environmentally conscious cities. It offered high walkability, access to bicyclists, farm-to-table dining, with loads of public parks.

I realized I was hungry, becoming sleepy, and needed a bathroom. I located a restaurant. Afterwards, I noticed a Starbucks. A gym was less than two miles away, along with a Wal-Mart about seven miles away. It was the trifecta. Most likely, the Wal-Mart would be that night's home. It was almost 7:30 p.m. Purchasing a hotel room seemed pointless. I decided to take advantage of the WiFi to research spots to perform. My friend was arriving on Monday. I wanted to stay in the same hotel or near him. I was planning to remain in Portland until Tuesday morning, then possibly head back toward the coast to Astoria.

My dream was writing musical lyrics, books, and blogs which allowed me to see castles where other people lived. I desired to travel to their lands.

I had noticed on the "Confessions of a Dreamer Tour," when I shared my dreams, I saw a gaze in other people's eyes. A desire their dreams were still alive. They might have had to bury them under the burden of struggling for water to drink, food to eat, or the same place to sleep every night, but they were there. I believed anything and everything was possible. I was choosing to run hungry every day to pursue my bliss. I trusted limits only existed in the mind.

"When you know what you want, and want it bad enough, you will find a way to get it" – Jim Rohn.

To those individuals who have desired to accomplish something but decided to bury it, I simply say: "Just start." Ask yourself what makes you happy. Then do it every day even if only for 5 – 10 minutes. The next thing you notice, you might be doing it daily for a wealth you could only dream about. Keep dreaming. There are no limits. Continue to believe in yourself. Live your life like you could not fail.

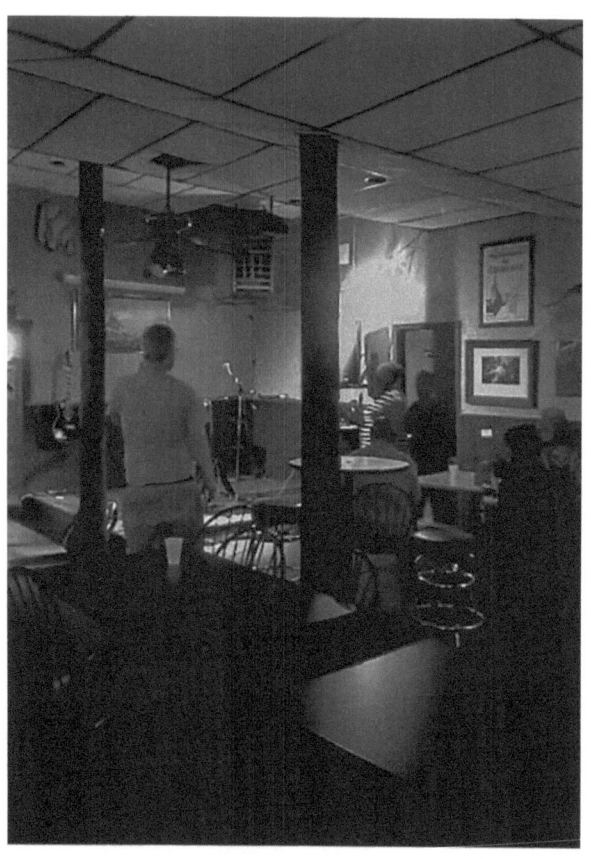

Firkin Tavern
Portland, Oregon

CHAPTER 38

APRIL 17, 2016

I did not sleep well that night. I was exhausted from the adventure of the day before. I thought I would crash easily. I did fall asleep quickly. Unfortunately, it was only a power nap of 30 minutes. Afterward, I was awake for almost two hours. I gazed upon the clock, 1:00 a.m., 2:00 a.m. Then finally around 3:00 a.m., I drifted asleep again. I awoke around 7:30 a.m. I attempted to remain in the backseat for another hour to no avail. I gave up on the notion to continue sleeping. Instead, I drove to a McDonald's. I enjoyed a breakfast of hotcakes and sausage. I used their free WiFi to catch up on email and social media. I decided on a haircut. It had been about six weeks since the last one. I was getting shaggy. The problem was I was always quite particular about haircuts. I searched online to locate a walk-in establishment with the highest customer reviews from Yelp. I normally had a personal stylist with whom I forged a relationship and trusted, so simply walking into a barbershop or similar establishment was a big step for me.

I walked into a Portland's version of a Supercuts. It was highly recommended on Yelp. When the lady asked how I wanted my hair cut, I told her scissors over comb and if possible, to please use a razor to texturize it. She stated she had done hair for over 30 years and had never heard of the technique. I became nervous and almost walked out. Though apprehensive, I decided to remain. Through our conversation, she did everything I desired. I guess she just had other names for the techniques. Besides, I did not let her cut off too much hair. Rather, she performed a basic clean-up. She did a very good job. I exited the shop feeling pleased.

Before checking into the hotel, I spent about an hour riding around the city in the truck. Portland struck me as an interesting city with a hip vibe and lots to do. Perhaps it was even a place to live in the future.

I checked into the hotel, the Quality Inn Downtown Convention Center. It was located next to the hotel my friend Matt and his mom would be staying in when they flew into town the next day to visit some of his friends. The hotel was not 5-star, but it offered a bed, a hot shower, safe parking, and, at less than $75 a night. It was a blessed treat.

After I checked in. I walked around a few blocks to check out the neighborhood. It was a brief walk. Honestly,

I spent most of the day lounging in bed watching TV. After I returned from the quick walk. I searched the internet for places to perform. I was able to locate a venue called Firkin Tavern located about two miles away from the hotel. I hadn't performed anywhere since I was in Long Beach, California.

Firkin Tavern was a small bar. There were about 15 people in the audience. The Portland Trailblazers were on the TVs because they were in the NBA playoffs. I met a guy from Canada, Scott, who lived in Portland. He played the alto sax. He had been attending the open mic for a few weeks. Scott said it was one of the better ones in Portland.

When I walked onto the stage for the three-song set, I introduced myself and explained my journey as well as why I was there. The audience applauded. I performed the three songs with each one receiving applause. As I was performing the set, the Trailblazers were mounting a comeback from a deficit. So, maybe the applause was for them instead. Unfortunately, no one purchased an autographed CD. Nonetheless, it was swell to perform anyway. I had fun.

Scott asked me to sing and perform during his set as he played the sax. We created a few easy songs from my list he knew and could harmonize on easily. We performed my favorite Eddie Vedder song, "Hard Sun," a Marshal Tucker Band song, "Can't You See," and an original of mine, "Crossroads." I had never performed with a sax player. Someone from the audience videotaped our set. The performance floats around on YouTube along with my Facebook page for Tommy Ray Music.

At the close of the open mic, Scott invited me to another place on Monday night. He said it was the best open mic in Portland. He told me to arrive early. It was restricted to a certain number of performers. On most Monday nights, there was a line waiting to sign up. I returned to the hotel. I discovered the open mic bar Scott had just recommended, The Goodfoot, was already on the list I had compiled beforehand as one of the places I had desired to perform. I enjoyed the comforts of a long hot shower and a bed. A good night's sleep was on the horizon as I watched some cable TV. I thought about plans for the next day. I was truly grateful. Gratitude was growing deep inside of me during the whole tour, overflowing.

As my head was supported by the pillow, the warm covers embracing my body, I sensed I had the qualities and the strengths required to do what I planned. *I was accomplishing great things in my life. "To preserve is favorable" – Warrior of the Light. I had the creative power, the positive energy I needed.*

Always remember readers, you are on a journey of success. You may be approached by haters, including your own family. Do not allow them to drag you down. You have your vision, your goals as well as the desire. Persevere through their negative talk. Keep striving, never stop on your dreams. Never give up. Have faith you're moving forward. Continue telling

APRIL 17, 2016

yourself, why not? What do you have to lose? A short-term of pain and roughness may occur, though it could lead you to a future of your dreams. Keep your positive mindset. "The mind is everything. What you think you become" – Buddha.

At times, you may become tired. You may be physically or emotionally drained. Keep going. Fight through it. Be the one who sees things which don't exist. You are a creative being. Utilize your imagination. Do not worry or stress about the how. Never surrender. You may feel fear. Do it anyways.

Best wishes on changing your life. You make each day amazing by chasing your dreams. Feel the joy inside of you as you chase your dreams. You may have to work all day at a day job. Do your best to come home and spend the time needed doing what you love. You are amazing. Enjoy your true passion.

Remember! Some of the greats said it's never too late. An example is Colonel Sanders. He was in his 60s when he started KFC. I know you have greatness inside of you. Listen to your inner voice. Trust your instincts. Set your mind to win. Have faith. Hold on. Keep grinding.

So, what will you do?

The Goodfoot
Portland, Oregon

CHAPTER 39

APRIL 18, 2016

I had been sleeping in the back seat of the truck off and on for a month. At the hotel, I slept until almost 10:30 a.m. The bed was like a soft cloud. I had to use inner force and my desire to see more of Portland as fuel to climb out from the cloud. I could have easily laid in the bed the entire day.

I researched on the internet for a bookstore. There was a Barnes & Noble about a half mile away. I needed a new journal. Instead of driving, I thought I would take a stroll there. It was a beautiful day outside, with blue skies and the temperature in the low 80s. It had been about two weeks since the weather was so lovely. The past two weeks had been mostly grey with rain and temperatures in the 50s. As I walked the sidewalk, I thought it would be a wonderful idea to grab some lunch at a local café… perhaps a café offering seating outside to people watch.

As I entered the establishment, I heard someone call my name from behind. I turned around, wondering who knew me in Portland. I discovered it was my friend Jason. Jason was my roommate back in 2006 in Hilton Head Island, South Carolina. He had been in Portland for the past three weeks setting up his business, Orange Fitness. He told me he would be flying home to Atlanta the next day. It was glorious catching up with Jason, sharing how our lives had unfolded over the past decade. We probably talked for about an hour over lunch before we had to go our separate ways. Jason had always been an inspiration to me, and I was happy he was doing so well.

At moments, the world seemed so large and vast. In another moment, it was tiny. I think the Universe did it in one's life for special reasons.

The mission at Barnes & Nobles was to purchase a new journal. When I was shopping, a high school buddy, David, called me. He asked about the tour and offered me a great opportunity. He wanted to know if I would perform at our 25th High School Reunion in Lexington, North Carolina for Central Davidson Senior High School. I agreed and told him I would figure out the details about how to get there later. I was truly honored to be asked.

After the trip to Barnes & Nobles, I introduced myself to a street busker. He was the first daytime street performer I had seen on my adventures. I asked his opinion of Portland and how he was doing performing on the streets. He said Portland was open to street performing in multiple locations. He did not have a permit. He said he had had minimal hassles from the police. He was playing his guitar through the same type of amp I owned, but singing without a microphone. I thought about staying another day and trying to busk on the streets somewhere myself.

I received another phone call. The call was from my friend Matt from Pittsburgh, the one who was flying into town later in the day. He told me he would not arrive until 10:30 p.m. I thought about staying another night so I could visit with him. Another day in Portland could offer a street busking performance and perhaps another opportunity to perform at an open mic if one was available.

After walking around the area, I returned to the motel to relax and prepare for the open mic later.

When I arrived at The Goodfoot, the doors were not yet open. It was about 6:30 p.m. The musicians were already lining up outside, waiting. I introduced myself to two other solo artists while we were waiting. One gentleman had been living in Portland about two years. The other was a newbie, there for only about two weeks. Around 7:05 p.m. the red door opened to a hallway where a guy was sitting on a stool. It cost two dollars to enter. Inside, the bar was dimly lit with candles burning on the table tops. There were sofa type seats, tables with chairs, and a center bar area with bar stools. I was told they offered a great selection of craft beers. The stage was decorated with lights containing a full band set-up. The Goodfoot offered a soundman. His sound booth was next to the bar on the other side of the room from the stage. One outstanding aspect: there was not a single TV in the place. People came to The Goodfoot to hear music, period.

The sign-up sheets were on the main bar. One could sign up for a time slot from 7:30 p.m. to 9:00 p.m. or from 9:00 p.m. to 10:30 p.m. Once one signed up for either time slot, one's name was written on the slip of paper. It was placed into a fish bowl and names were drawn out randomly. The slip of paper also indicated whether one had paid extra to have the house band play along or have the 10-minute session recorded. I chose the latter time slot thinking more people would be present. It created a higher probability to share my story as well as give myself the best opportunity to sell some EPs.

Of the first six artists who performed, two were talented. The others made me wonder why their songs had to be so long.

I was blessed. My name was drawn first for the second set. There were about 30 people in the bar. I stood under the lights. I shared my story. I performed three original songs, all to applause. The bright red lights on the stage made it difficult to see out into the audience. The sound was the best I had heard in a long time. I thought I had paid for a recording of my performance. Unfortunately, it did not happen. Either they did not see it on the form or I forgot to mark "Yes".

I remained there until about 11:00 p.m. I listened to all the acts and enjoyed the music. The terrific feature about the open mic was the diversity of performers. One performer played a violin, while his partner was on the keyboards. There was a guy rapping, a jazz band. I recorded some of the evening and showcased it on my Facebook music page.

I had been told by multiple people there and through my internet research the Goodfoot was the best open mic in Portland. I was grateful I had the opportunity to perform there. After I departed, I was hungry. I made the poor choice of ordering some garbage fast food again. I returned to the motel.

My friend's plane was delayed. It did not land until almost midnight. The delayed flight caused him and his mom to miss the show. We made plans to catch up the next day.

I drifted asleep in the cloud bed happy, joyous. Tonight, had reminded me how much I liked being on a stage, traveling, writing, and living my dream!

Have you ever had déjà vu? The term was French. It literally means "already seen." Those who have experienced the feeling described it as an overwhelming sense of familiarity.

"A Warrior of the Light knows certain moments repeat themselves. He often finds himself faced by the same problems and situations, seeing the difficult situations return. He

grows depressed. Thinking that he was incapable of making any progress in life, his heart speaks, 'I've been through all of this before.' Yes, you have been through all this before, replied the heart. But you have never been beyond it. Then the Warrior of the Light realized those repeated experiences have but one aim. To teach him what he does not want to learn"
– Paulo Coelho.

Trust your inner voice. If your personal déjà vu occurs, ensure it was not actually a lesson to be taught. Have faith the Universe was ready to step in and assist you. I believe you can reach beyond your limits.

The Columbia River
Astoria, Oregon

CHAPTER 40
APRIL 19, 2016

When I awoke, I almost decided to remain another night in Portland. The only reason I did not was there were no open mic opportunities on Tuesdays. I could have stayed and attempted to street-busk, sight-see, or catch up on reading and writing. Rather, I decided to leave Portland after visiting with my friend.

I packed my belongings and loaded the silver truck I called home. I checked out of the hotel and walked over to meet Matt and his mom. It was fantastic catching up. I had not seen Matt since PA school in Savannah, Georgia. We graduated in early 2009. I spent so much time alone. It was wonderful to interact with someone, share a conversation, and laugh. It was the same thing on my Camino de Santiago trip in 2012. I was alone most of the way. I cherished the moments when I could interact with others.

Matt assured me I was doing the right thing as he told me he had been reading my blogs and posts. My journey had instilled in him the belief he should follow his passions and loves which were also not in medicine. I gave him one year to at least start chasing his dreams part-time. I recalled the scene from Fight Club when Brad Pitt put the gun to the head of the store clerk. He told him if he wasn't following his dreams in six months, he was going to die. He said, "the next morning the guy would awaken to the most beautiful day of his life." I told Matt he did not have to jump all in. In fact, it was probably best if he didn't, unless he had saved a nest egg or had his plans to pursue his dreams already in place. I would say the same to anyone considering giving up what was considered a "normal" life to go after their dreams. Plan, save, and take baby steps at first.

If one were constantly stressed about money and did not have the mentality of abundance and prosperity, one's dreams might die before one even got started. I had faith in myself. I believed my dreams were already there and the goals I had set were already accomplished. I could live each day in abundance and prosperity.

With the above said, I was not prospering as I had planned through street busking. The original plan was to earn at least $20 a day. The cost of fuel, eating, and using motels/hotels was more than anticipated. I needed to be prepared financially for those times. The financial plan I had chosen was the following: I cashed out the re-

APRIL 19, 2016

tirement fund from the position I held at Mississippi College. It provided almost $8,000 after taxes and penalties. I had a credit card with $8,000 cash limit. I had deferred school loans.

The cash allowed three months of strategic living expenses to cover mandatory bills along with a small amount of cash once the tour was concluded. I was blessed as well. I knew I had family I could stay with in Mississippi and in Florida for free upon my return. It allowed me an opportunity to think about the next move after Rambling Across America.

After a marvelous visit, I departed my friend around noon. I returned to the road again, headed west towards Astoria. The distance would cover almost 100 miles.

As I drove, I noticed something was wrong with the truck. I believed the tire balance was off, perhaps from the rough roads I had been driving on to locate camp sites. The steering wheel began to vibrate in my hands once I reached 40 to 50 mph. About an hour into the trip, I stopped at a tire store to inquire about a tire rotation and balance. Unfortunately, they could not perform the inspection right away. I did not want to lose any more of the day by waiting. Instead, I continued the road to Astoria.

The plan was to find a state park on the other side of Astoria, spend the night, then make my way to Seattle, Washington the next day.

The fascinating thing I noticed when entering Astoria was the water. There was a thick mist over the water reaching up a few hundred feet with the mountains in the background. It was eerie. It reminded me of the movie *The Fog*. The town itself was unique. It offered lots of harbor points, taverns and bars, along with plenty of local restaurants. I stopped and snapped a few photographs. I noticed a concrete slab about 100 yards long filled with seals sun-bathing. They were barking at each other loudly. I stood there to listen to their song for a few moments.

Before heading to the Fort Stevens State Park, I stopped at a local grocery store to restock supplies. I was blessed. The supermarket offered free internet, a rarity for grocery stores on the tour. I sat down for a few minutes in their café and updated e-mail along with social media.

Resupplied, I drove to the state park. Evening approached. I noticed the fog was increasing and temperatures dropping. Like much of the northwest weather I had encountered. The evening was going to be in the low 40s, perhaps even a rain shower or two.

When I reached the state park, it was about five times larger than any other state park I had visited. I was delighted. It offered lots of mountain biking trails and other interesting stuff to see, like a shipwreck. When I checked the accommodations. I learned they had only seven tent sites, but over 200 hundred sites for RVs. I drove through the small tent section. I saw two empty spots. I thought, "Great! For $21, I'll have a place to stay, make a fire, grill the pork chop I bought, and take a few hits of my Oregon herb." When I returned to the ranger station, he told me all the tent sites were already taken. He mentioned I could stay in an RV spot for $29. I have done it before. But with the temperatures in the low 40s and rain a possibility, I decided instead to obtain a hotel room back in Astoria.

I used the Hotel.com app to inquire what hotels were near and check their rates. There were only two hotels under $80 with excellent reviews. I choose a hotel which the app stated was 12 miles away. However, it was actually 25 miles away. It was also in the State of Washington.

On the way towards Long Beach, Washington, where the hotel was. I had to cross over an unusual bridge, the Astoria-Megler Bridge. The architecture was phenomenal. It passed over the waterway connecting Oregon and Washington. The bridge offered views of hundreds of miles of shoreline. It seemed to be low tide as well. The fog and mist created a creepy, horror movie theme as I drove over it. It was funny, when halfway across, the GPS announced, "Welcome to Washington." I almost jumped out of my skin.

On the state of Washington side, I noticed how the shoreline was drastically different than the Pacific Highway course from California to Oregon. There were no cliffs, no rocks, simply water. It reminded me of the Gulf of Mexico I was used to when I lived above Clearwater,

Florida, from 2009 to 2012. As I entered Long Beach, the fog increased; a heavy mist in the air.

I located the hotel. A quaint little cottage style building. It offered a comfortable bed, cable TV with internet, and a hot shower for less than $80 a night. After checking in, I drove through the town to see what it had to offer. The town itself was a whimsical little beach town. Shops lined the streets on both sides. I noticed an arcade filled with games for the kids, fudge shops, and plenty of places to purchase souvenirs.

I researched open mics or singer/songwriter venues for Astoria and Long Beach. Unfortunately, I could not find any. Instead, I decided to focus on my writing and reading. I looked at the map and saw I was only three hours shy of Seattle. I didn't realize it was so close. I wanted to thoroughly check out the city of Seattle. I was planning to stay there up to three nights. Most likely it meant three nights in a hotel.

The "Confessions of a Dreamer Tour" continued with bliss, happiness, and faith. Something I just recalled: as I was leaving Portland, I observed a billboard sign saying, "Follow Your Heart."

"A warrior does not spend his days trying to play the role others have chosen for him" – Paulo Coelho.

I believed there was nothing more powerful than being original. Not conforming to what others thought you should do. I hope you look at your life and smile knowing your facing your fears. It may vary from person to person. It may mean you chose a pathway toward a certain dream, listening to a genre of music, a fashion choice, or your love.

Some may call you stupid. You may not choose to attend college, spend hours on Facebook, or watch the latest TV shows. You have the power to control your footsteps. Walk the pathway you choose for the adventure we call life.

I suggest you keep moving forward towards your goals, desires, as well as your dreams. What's the worst could happen? You fail. So what, Benjamin Franklin failed 1000 times. If you have the strength for your journey, do not stop grinding each day.

The task may be hard. Many may not try. Your EGO may attempt to talk you out of it with negative talk. Focus on your potential. If the doors always seemed closed for your path, simply take a sledgehammer to the wall and create your own door. Always believe in yourself. You may be the only one who does. Do not waste your life with regrets. Push through it. Act on the plan you created.

I began my new plan in May 2014. I was striving for my goals. Each day I took a new baby step. Some days I could leap. I continued to have unwavering faith and purpose by acting in a certain way. I maintained patience. I decided I would rather walk along the current journey than a 9 to 5 job for a paycheck.

Keep telling yourself nothing can stop you. Remain confident you are accomplishing your goals. Believe your thoughts create your reality.

Partial Whale Skeleton
Long Beach, Washington

CHAPTER 41

APRIL 20, 2016

Long Beach was known for its beach and boardwalk on the Long Beach Peninsula. Colorful kites were on show at the World Kite Museum. The Discovery Trail traced a coastal route taken by explorers Lewis and Clark. At the mouth of the Columbia River, the 1800s Cape Disappointment and North Head lighthouses overlooked the Pacific Ocean. Willapa National Wildlife Refuge had bird-rich wetlands.

I awoke and savored the comfortable bed. I watched the clock tick closer to the check-out time of 11:00 a.m. I thought about staying another night. I looked at the weather report. It predicted cloudy skies and temperatures in the high 50s. I gazed upon the desk with its stack of books. I knew I needed to get caught up with my reading and writing. I thought about the choices. I could remain there another night at the hotel or drive about 10 minutes south to the state park or drive an hour plus north to another state park. As 11:00 a.m. approached, I contacted the front desk and asked the clerk if I could stay until noon to give me more time to reach a decision. I used the time to write in my journal. I sensed I was hitting another wall of fatigue, but I was not giving up on the tour or performing. Simply, I decided to indulge and spoil myself. I decided to stay another night in the hotel. The room was cozy. The beach town was quaint. It allowed me to spend the day writing and reading.

I embarked on an hour stroll through the town as well as to the ocean. The landscape was completely different there. The sand was still the darker color common to the Northwest. The shoreline was almost flat with no cliffs or rock formations. There were small waves rolling in. I noticed one could not camp on the beach, though I saw people parked on the beach with tents for the day. It was permitted to have fires on there as well. The idea of a campfire on the beach appealed to me. It seemed it was never allowed in the coastal towns where I had lived: Hilton Head Island, South Carolina or Palm Harbor, Florida. The ability to have a fire on the beach reminded me of the opening scene of the movie *Jaws*. There was a long boardwalk in both directions where people were strolling and enjoying nature. I noticed a few bike paths along the beach I thought I might try later. After eating a donut and buying some homemade fudge, I headed back to the room to focus on my writing. I accomplished three hours of work. To allow a mental break, I decided to enjoy the ocean breeze by opening the room's window and taking a justified nap. When I awoke, I wrote for another hour before I decided to head out for some dinner.

Unfortunately, I had mistreated my body over the past two weeks. I had made poor food choices with no exercise from a weight lifting standpoint. I was truly blessed considering I still felt and looked healthy. I had eaten mostly fried food along with fast food, and limited vegetables. It was completely different than my normal diet.

I emailed a contact in Seattle, Washington to inquire about places to perform in the city. He told me about a place I could perform the next two nights. I still had not yet decided if I would get a hotel or spend the first night in Seattle in the truck. I didn't know where in Seattle I wanted to stay. I noticed when I checked on Hotels.com, they had multiple listings for Seattle hotels based on what attractions one wanted to visit. I spoke to a couple of people to get their ideas. I researched key locations in Seattle. I decided to stick to my usual plan of finding a Starbucks and a Wal-Mart.

I contemplated staying three full nights in Seattle. The city offered open mics seven nights a week. Besides, I needed to shop for my black-tie outfit for the Mississippi Foundation Music Awards show where I would be walking my first red carpet.

After a Chinese dinner, I was on my way back to the night's dwelling place when I walked by an Arcade. The child inside of me could not resist. I entered and put a $10 bill through the token machine. I played on games from childhood before moving up to the 4D games. One game was horror themed. I was enclosed in curtains as I stood with my weapon, shooting zombies. The surrounding speakers intensified the drama. At times, I thought a monster was behind me. It was quite intense.

Upon my return to the hotel, I decided to have a quiet evening. A few moments of a movie I had seen numerous times led to a deep sleep.

Sunset
Long Beach, Washington

CHAPTER 42
APRIL 21, 2016

I awoke in Long Beach, Washington, again. No, it was not my own Groundhog Day. I was simply tired. Furthermore, laying in the bed was remarkable. I was truly grateful to be wrapped up in a blanket, stretched out. I slept until 10:00 a.m. I had to leave in an hour due to the 11:00 a.m. checkout time. After contemplating the options again, such as departing and heading towards Seattle or driving an hour north to camp at a state park, I decided to remain in Long Beach for the day. I could enjoy biking, laundry, and watching my last sunset over the Pacific Ocean before heading up to Seattle and then back towards the East Coast for Mississippi.

I repacked the truck and checked out. I drove to the beach and parked. In one direction on the boardwalk was an eight-mile bike ride ending at a lighthouse. The opposite direction had a two-mile trail. I first rode along the two-mile trail to the end and returned to the parking area of the truck. Then, I rode four miles the opposite direction. Overall, I went for a ten-mile bike ride along the ocean. It was an enjoyable ride, though most of the trail was behind the sand dunes, which hid the ocean from view. During the bike ride on their boardwalk, I was startled as I came over one hill to see a snake crossing the bike path. Luckily, it did not startle me enough to crash my bike. I had been known to even be startled while driving my truck when seeing a snake on the road.

After the bike ride, I walked to a small pavilion by the ocean which offered picnic tables and grills. I was going to use it for a time for reading and writing. When I sat down at a table, the temperature became so chilly I started to shiver. I returned to the truck's driver seat. I had six hours until the sunset. Over the next six hours, I did what I told myself I did not want to do. I drove around killing time. I drove to one state park south of me. However, I did not stop to visit since I would have to pay a fee to park. I returned towards Long Beach again. While I drove through those different areas, my cell phone would have service for a few moments, then would lose service. I found myself trying to find hot spots so I could use my phone. I chose to return to the beach area where some public restrooms were. The one highlight of the day happened by those public restrooms. For about an hour, I watched two deer eat and relax by the high grass of the dunes near the ocean. They were much larger than the deer we had in Mississippi, each being well over 125 pounds. Their fur was also different, shaggy almost.

As the evening finally approached, negative thoughts seeped into my mind. Utilizing positive affirmations, I enjoyed a lovely sunset over the Pacific Ocean. I knew all decisions had consequences. My decision to remain in Long Beach meant I had to leave in the dark, which also meant I was missing out on seeing all the beautiful scenery along the way from Long Beach towards Seattle. During the one-and-a-half-hour drive to Aberdeen, Washington, I could only see what my truck lights illuminated. Driving on those curvy roads at night was quite an adventure. I passed through a few towns and could tell I was missing out on something amazing along the shoreline to my left.

As I arrived in Aberdeen, I located a Wal-Mart. It would be my home for the night. I arrived there about 11:00 p.m. I had considered stopping earlier in one of those small towns I had passed, but I was afraid I would not fall asleep quickly. Driving through to the city of Aberdeen placed me at my destination close to the time I had normally been going to bed.

The Wal-Mart offered WiFi in the parking lot. I located a parking spot where I was safe. I prepared myself and the truck for sleep. It was almost a week since I had used a Wal-Mart parking lot. I stealthily moved into position in the backseat. I closed my eyes on another day of the "Confessions of a Dreamer Tour." Gratitude continued to spill over into my psyche. *I was seeing parts of the country I had longed to see for years. Their beauty was overwhelming.*

As I lay on the pillow, I asked myself, "Am I the one?" Paulo Coelho wrote once, "If you are the one, you set out on your journey. You may feel cowardly. You may not always make the right decisions. You may suffer over the most trivial things. You may not believe you are capable of growing. You may feel unworthy of any blessing or miracle. You may not always be quite sure of what you are doing here. You may have sleepless nights. You may believe your life has no meaning. This is why you are the one. You make mistakes. You ask yourself questions. You are always looking for the reason. You are sure to find it."

Perhaps you are working a day job then at night pursuing your goals, desires, and dreams. Perhaps you perform covers at the bar as you compose your originals. Perhaps you do many things for others to fund your goals. Keep doing what you must. Keep pursuing your goals, desires, and your dreams daily. I understand you might be tired after working all day. Keep grinding. You must keep dreaming. Feel the confidence burning inside of you. Continue your focus. Remain positive in all you do. Stay ambitious.

Acting on your dreams separates you from being just a dreamer or wishful thinker. Set your goals, create a plan, and act to complete them. Desire to win big. Do not look back. Strive to keep your focus. Let your creativity shine bright. Do not quit. I would rather die in trying than live a life of regret of not trying.

APRIL 21, 2016

Watch videos, read books, and find others who are doing what you desire. Ask for guidance. Be limitless. Enjoy your journey.

Seattle, Washington

CHAPTER 43

APRIL 22, 2016

I drifted to sleep quickly last night. Sadly, I awoke several times throughout the night. I had four to six dreams. They awoke me each time. I could recall bits and pieces of them. A rainstorm started. It lasted most of the night. The noise of the rain drops upon the truck woke me a few times as well. When I awoke the first time, I thought it was already morning. I guessed it was due to sleeping so deeply. Unfortunately, it turned out it was only about an hour after I first fell asleep. The blessing of the evening was the parking lot itself was very quiet, which helped.

I awoke to a misting grey sky. I put on my flip flops and entered the store. After visiting the Wal-Mart to use the bathroom, brush my teeth along with breakfast at the inside McDonald's, I departed Aberdeen. I began the drive to Seattle. At that junction in my travels, I was comfortable using a Wal-Mart bathroom like it was my own.

The road to Seattle was pleasant. I drove into town by an enchanting river. As I approached the city of Seattle, I decided to use Hotels.com to book a hotel for a few days. I located a hotel near the port and the professional stadium used by the Seattle Seahawks. The one thing I did not know was the hotel did not offer free parking. I was charged an extra $25 a day for a parking garage a couple of blocks away from the hotel.

When I was checked in, my first desire was to take a nap. The weather outside was gloomy and in the mid-50s. The nap turned out to be almost three hours long. After I awoke, I checked my email. I found an email from a fan of Tommy Ray Music. He had found me on Reverbnation.com. It turned out he was performing a few miles away. I ventured out to watch him perform and to say hello. He had been performing for about 15 months. His lack of experience showed. I admired him for getting out there and trying. He was 60 years old. He proved my belief it was never too late to chase dreams, to follow bliss. A year earlier, I would never have thought I would meet a fan of my music over 3000 miles away from my home base of Mississippi. I now had fans from other parts of the world listening to Tommy Ray Music.

I had planned to remain in Seattle until Monday morning. Unfortunately, things were not looking promising. It was too cold, and the daily threat of rain meant no street busking. I was told about open mics on Mondays through Thursdays where I could perform. Per a web-

APRIL 22, 2016

site I located, there were some places I could perform on Saturday and Sunday as well. I met a guy who told me if I performed Monday night at an open mic, he would come out and listen to me. He took my information off my Facebook page, Tommy Ray Music. So, my plans were to check out of the hotel on Monday and enjoy the day until I performed. I was performing at an open mic at The Hard Rock Café - Seattle. Upon my departure from Seattle, I decided I would most likely locate a Wal-Mart parking lot and begin the long journey east on Tuesday.

Downtown
Seattle, Washington

CHAPTER 44

APRIL 23, 2016

Last night, the cars on the freeway I was next to sounded like waves from the ocean. It was soothing. The bed was super cozy with its sheets and blankets. It brought me into a deep slumber.

When I next saw the clock, it was 6:30 a.m. I was beginning to think it should be my wakeup time every day. But usually, I forced myself to sleep longer, until 8:30 a.m. or 9:00 a.m.

I took advantage of the blue-sky day in Seattle to walk the downtown streets. I wanted to see as much of the city on foot as I could. I did have a few things I desired to accomplish. I needed to purchase a red-carpet outfit to wear to the awards show and locate a music store to purchase a new guitar strap. On the streets of Seattle, it was in the 60s, with blue skies which were a true blessing. It was a delightful day. I first walked to the Pike Place

Market, about a mile from the hotel. As I entered, I wandered through the crowed aisles. It reminded me of Redding Square Market in Philly. It was the same concept: a large, open public market filled with vendors selling everything from fresh seafood, meat, baked goods, fruit and vegetables, as well as arts and crafts. There were lots of little restaurants offering plenty of appetizing items to eat and drink. I did not spend a lot of time inside of the market, since it was crowded and difficult to walk around all the tourists.

Whenever I visited a city, even for the first time, I found myself attempting to walk around like a local. I kept my head down. I wove in and out of slower-moving tourists. If I chose to snap photographs, I was sneaky about it. I thought those tactics reduced the chance of being targeted.

Next, I went looking for a suit to wear for the Mississippi Music Awards show in early May. I had been told Seattle was on the cutting edge of fashion compared to much of the East Coast. The first place I visited was Kuhlman's, on First Avenue. They had a great Yelp rating. I looked through the store but all they had was one Italian cut suit on their rack. It was a straightforward black suit with no bling. So, I exited and went off to the next place called Ian's, but they did not carry black-tie attire. Butch, the store manager, told me Kuhlman's was the best tailor in town. He said any off-the-rack suit at Kuhlman's would be well worth the purchase price. He glanced at my list of possible men's stores I wanted to visit and added a couple more. I exited his store and headed off to the third store. Oddly, I realized I had turned the wrong way. I had walked almost a half a mile on foot the wrong direction. I noticed I was walking in the direction of the Kuhlman store. I considered it fate. There, I discussed the options for the on-the-rack suit. They had me try on the black Italian suit. He mentioned the tailoring needs. The suit basically fit properly. Based on Butch's advice and because of the great basic fit, I purchased the suit from Kuhlman's. It was my first custom-tailored black suit. In the past, I'd always bought suits off a sales rack in a department store. Now I would have a custom-tailored black Italian suit lasting me until the end of time, with proper care. It was more than worth the $650 I paid. The tailor told me his custom suits from scratch are about $2,000. I'd really found a bargain.

The next mission was to find a guitar store to purchase a new guitar strap. There was supposed to be one in Pike Place Market. However, it turned out the guy was a day vendor. He crafted soap-box guitars. When I called him, he provided some advice about the music scene in Seattle. It included where I could go to perform on the streets safely. I told him I would visit him before I departed town to check out his creations. I located the guitar store he mentioned, Emerald Guitars. It was an impressive, locally-owned music store. The store had two left-handed guitars for sale, a rarity in my personal experience. They had an acoustic and an electric...a special treat, a 1972 Gibson. The owner was pleasant and gracious. We talked about my current tour and dreams of songwriting and performing.

The weather remained gorgeous as I left the guitar store. After walking for about four hours, it was time to head back to the hotel. I decided to either write or take a nap. I was learning when I stayed in a hotel I did not get much done because of the TV and the bed. Since the rooms had WiFi, it allowed more time online. I could send email, blog, and post to social media, but it took away from reading, writing, or practicing. When I left Seattle Monday night or Tuesday morning, I would need to camp out more to avoid those distractions.

After a long nap, I tried to do some reading and writing. It was around 7:30 p.m. I decided it was time for some dinner. As I stepped outside the hotel, the first thing I noticed was the more typical Seattle weather had returned with falling temperatures, wind, and a mist of rain. I entered a local eatery to have a sandwich for dinner. I found the rain had increased when I finished dinner. It was hard enough! I headed back to the hotel instead of checking out the area after dark or going to a bar for a drink. I smoked some herb as I walked back to the hotel. Marijuana was legal there. I was taking tokes in public just like someone smoking a regular cigarette. I had read an article explaining how the City of Seattle was more interested in issuing tickets for jay-walking than in people smoking marijuana in public. Knowing I desired to write still, I took a few tokes on the walk to see if I would feel any extra creative response.

Once again, I did not feel it did much of anything for me. When I first entered the room, I noticed some blurred vision when I was trying to read. I attempted to finish my reading of inspirational pages. Unfortunately, the temptation of the TV was too grand. I stopped writing and picked up my guitar. As the TV played, I strummed softly with my fingertips for about an hour.

I researched locations to perform the next night. I planned to visit the waterfront, perhaps even ride my bike around. Most of the day I planned to simply be a tourist.

I hoped my writing would inspire my readers to get out and follow their dreams, always.

A major reason I took the leap of faith for the "Confession of a Dreamer Tour" was two-fold. First was the dream. Second, I was listening to my heart. At first, it seemed difficult listening to my heart. I maintained faith and persisted. I believed I was creating a channel for higher wisdom. I trusted my heart had a personal message just for me. A message only I could hear. I learned the voice of my heart calmed my mind. It overshadowed the negative EGO talk.

I ask you to sit quietly, listen to your own heart. Shut out the distractions. I know you have what it takes. Continue to remain creative. Use your imagination as a child. Create value in our world. Your heart provides you the strength to confront your fears. Never give up, my friends.

Conor Byrne Pub
Seattle, Washington

CHAPTER 45
APRIL 24, 2016

I awoke to a typical Seattle day. The temperature was in the 40s with overcast skies along with rain. Nevertheless, I was not going to allow the weather to deter me from having a dynamite day. I had planned to stroll the wet streets. Later, I would be performing at Conor Byrne Pub.

I returned to the Pike Place Market. I wanted to introduce myself to Dean Moller, the owner of Soul Cat Guitars. In addition to building cigar box guitars, he also constructed amps out of cigar boxes. Quite ingenious. Dean demonstrated one of his 4-strings along with a 6-string model. He offered to let me play one. Unfortunately, since I am left-handed, I could not. Mr. Moller told me it takes about a week to build a 6-string model, and about two or three days for the 4-string version. Dean told me about some places where I could perform on the street which I hadn't heard about before through online research.

After speaking with Dean, I realized Seattle was a city I would enjoy visiting for at least a week or more perhaps relocating too. Seattle had also made the list of candidates for a possible future relocation.

As I walked away from the Market, the rain stopped and started periodically. Luckily, it was nothing too major. There were still lots of people walking around the streets of the city. Since I was singing later I chose not to remain out in the weather too long. I might be an amateur in people's eyes, but I treated my voice as a professional performer would. I protected it by following basic rules which I had learned through reading. A few techniques were to wear a scarf, to drink pineapple juice before singing, and when able, to take a hot steamy shower with facial stretching exercises. Even if I was only performing at an open mic, I protected my voice.

Back at the hotel, I lounged around and relaxed while watching TV. I practiced a few original songs and performed some voice exercises.

Later, I went to the Conor Byrne Pub. Per Google, the Conor Byrne Pub was one of Seattle's oldest watering holes. It was nestled in the heart of historical Ballard. It brought the city's finest beer, music, and atmosphere together as well as easily having the best pint of Guinness in town. I immensely relished the true Irish appearance with its long, old-fashioned wooden bar accompanying the draft taps lining the wall. The stage was classic. A chandelier hung from the ceiling with two lamp posts on either side. The pub itself had a wooden floor as well as wooden bench seats. When people walked by, I thought my butt might get pinched on the wood.

The open mic itself was sharp. Beasley, the open mic host, was running sound. In addition, I liked how he organized the set-up. He formed two groups. One group was composed of performers who had played there before. The other group consisted of first timers. He had a returning person pull a letter from a dark marble bag. He then signed them up based on the letter. Then he did the same routine with a newcomer. The letter allowed a person to pick the time slot. For example, an A was allowed to pick their time slot before those who drew the letter B. I signed up for 8:45 p.m. It was the fourth act of the first hour.

The atmosphere was perfect. The Pub dimmed the lights. Candles burned on the table tops. The TVs over the bar were powered off. People focused on the stage. Almost everyone inside was present for the singer-songwriter's performances. When my turn came. I shared the story of the "Confessions of a Dreamer Tour." I performed three original songs. After each completed song, the joy of applause filled the Pub's atmosphere. Applause was addicting. I always desired more of it.

It could be difficult performing at an open mic. When I was in the audience, even though we all had the same allotted time, some performers seem to go on too long. Yet when I was up there on stage, my time flew by like a short breath.

After I performed, I hung out for a few more hours with the hope of selling some *Crossroads* EPs. I listened to others take the stage. No matter their talent level, they all received positive support along with applause from the audience. I always attempted to perform when I thought I might have the largest crowd. It improved my chances of selling more EPs or hearing more applause along with gaining exposure. The Pub became busier after my performance.

As I remained seated or walked to the bar, I was congratulated throughout the night by others. I met a guy who used to live in Knoxville, Tennessee. He complimented me on my music. On my way out to exit, a gentleman stopped me. He donated to the "Confessions of a Dreamer Tour" by purchasing the EP of *Crossroads*. My music overall had received more praise on the West Coast than it did on the East Coast.

I exited the Pub and returned to the parking garage near the hotel. After I parked the truck, I went searching for some food. I was surprised everything was closed. By using Yelp, I found an open bar still serving food. I went to the J-H Café. The bartender was from Memphis, Tennessee, about three hours from where I lived in Mississippi. I shared with him my music and tour as I enjoyed a cheeseburger and fries. He mentioned I could return in a few days to perform there if I were still in town. Once a week they had an open stage jam session.

After eating, I returned to the hotel. I sat in the hotel room listening to the rain fall on a cold Seattle night.

I planned to perform the next night. After the performance, I would figure out the next move. Earlier, I'd met a guy from Pittsburgh at the Pub. He recommended I drive through Montana instead of taking a straight line to Salt Lake City. I had nine days of adventure remaining before I had to return to Mississippi for the awards show. I had to plan carefully to be sure I could make it back in time. Based on my calculations, it required 10 days to drive home if I only drove four to five hours per day.

The next day, I had to pick up the tailored Italian suit. I planned to check out of the hotel in the morning, kill the day sightseeing before I picked up the suit at 4:00 p.m., then I would go to the open mic to perform.

I loved Seattle. The city offered lots of the things I desired in a place to live. I had confidence I could break into the music scene there.

Downtown @ Night
Seattle, Washington

Conor Byrne Pub

CHAPTER 46

APRIL 25, 2016

Even though I could have remained in Seattle all week to perform at open mics. I knew I had to be disciplined. I had to begin the trek to the east to arrive at the awards ceremony on time. So, I checked out of the hotel.

I planned to sightsee most of the day, and if possible, catch up on reading and writing before picking up the suit at 4:00 p.m. I had to be at the Hard Rock Cafe around 5:00 p.m. to sign up for their open mic.

I chose not to indulge in my regular habit of driving around the city for hours and hours killing time and wasting gas. Instead, I visited the REI store. REI's home store was based in Seattle. It was a magical place. I could have stayed there all day. I could have outfitted all the adventure needs I had dreamed of, in one day. They offered almost everything in outdoor sports except surfing.

I remained in the store for more than an hour before moving on.

I then located a trusty Starbucks. I used their WiFi to post on social media and read some. I only needed to stay there about two hours. Since I had been in a hotel the past few days, I was not too far behind on those projects.

The Hard Rock Café - Seattle did not have its own parking lot. I had to park in a garage about a block away. The cost was $20 for the day. They closed at 11:00 p.m. The attendant mentioned if I returned after 11:00 p.m., I would have to call a special number to have the door opened.

The Hard Rock Café - Seattle was unparalleled to others. The stage was located upstairs in a place called The Cavern. When I walked up there, there was a duo act setting up to perform music from 5:00 p.m. to 7:00 p.m. I was told they had acts like them all week long. One way to be booked for the gig was to have an exceptional sound during one's open mic performance.

At 5:00 p.m., no customers were in The Cavern. I decided to remain to watch the duo perform. The Hard Rock offered a professional sound engineer. The stage was illuminated phenomenally, with multi-color lights. The duo was talented. It consisted of a guitarist and a violin player. After each song, the bartender and I clapped. I was taken aback not one other person was up there. It was happy hour. It remained empty the entire two hours the duo performed.

APRIL 25, 2016

The sign-up list was brought out. I placed my name on the list. I was able to meet the duo between sets. It turned out they were leaving the next day on their own quest to play music. They had already arranged some gigs during their trip to the east coast. They planned to be on the road almost four months. They were fun to talk to. We exchanged contact information, including our social media accounts. Through networking, we could boost each other's presence.

The other artists for the open mic arrived around 7:00 p.m. Close to 8:00 p.m., the open mic began. The acts included a trio using some computer backing to enhance their sound, a few rap/hip hop artists, two poets, as well as a handful of solo guitar players/singers like me. My time slot was about 9:00 p.m. I chose the time slot thinking it would be an excellent time when the most people would be on the premises. I followed the band. They were skilled, with a female lead singer, a gentleman on keyboards, a drummer and their laptop playing electric guitar backing tracks. They brought about 10 to 15 friends to hear them perform. Unfortunately, after they performed and returned to their seats, they all began to talk amongst themselves, which was distracting to the rest of us. The format of the open mic was two songs per performer. When it was my turn, there were probably about 20 people in front of me to hear the two original songs.

As I had done in the past, I told my story of the "Confessions of a Dreamer Tour." Positive energy flowed from the audience. I was confident and inspired. The 10 minutes went well. The sound was the best I had had so far. The addition of the dim lights on my red shirt created a rock star persona.

As I watched other acts after my turn, I began to ponder my night's plans for after the performance. I wondered how far I might be able to drive. I stuck around until 11:00 p.m. listening and hoping I might sell some *Crossroads* EPs. Though I had made no money, I was still following my bliss. I believed I had planted seeds to grow my dreams. I had successfully shared Tommy Ray Music to many new individuals.

I gathered my belongings and walked to the parking garage. Once I reached the top floor where I had parked the truck, I paused a moment to capture a few night shots of Seattle's downtown area. I decided to drive about an hour north to get out of the city, refuel, and eat dinner. I drove to the I-5 North. I set my compass to the Skagit Valley. It was on my list of must-see places. The region was well-known for its tulips. They even had a month-long tulip festival every Spring. People from around the world visited to drive through the fields of tulips. They also had special events scattered throughout the month.

I drove about a half hour short of the preplanned destination. I stopped to purchase fuel, ice, and to eat dinner. After the fast-food dinner, I searched for my haven,

APRIL 25, 2016

Wal-Mart. At the first one I located, I sat parked for about 20 minutes. Then I decided to move on because of the sights I was seeing around me. I did not feel safe.

I arrived at another Wal-Mart on the interstate further north. It offered increased lighting. Besides, other campers were there. I found a quiet space to park. It was going to be in the low 40s. I bundled up with layers of clothing to keep warm. They offered WiFi in the parking lot. I updated everything on social media.

As I cuddled up under the sleeping bag, I recalled previous readings. *It was once written you had a choice to choose your own enemies. Our primary enemy was ourselves through our self-negative talk. Another enemy may be our outward talk to others. I have learned there was no need to boast my qualities to others. I am confident I have the necessary gifts for my particular path.*

Nevertheless, we all know too well certain people exist. They fancy to boast and provoke others; they are able to do everything. They create a perception they are better than others. But instead of focusing on them, elect to focus on yourself. You have a destiny to fulfill.

As you prepare your journey, ensure you find the ways to take steps forward towards your goals. When not feeling your best, simply remember: "Wake up! If you knew you had a terminal illness, if you had little time left to live, you would not waste it. It is precious! I am telling you, you do have a terminal illness; it is called birth. So be happy now without reason or you never will be at all" – Dan Millman.

I want you to begin to feel urgency. Desire to live with creativity, focus, and love. Remain positive and optimistic. If others talk down to you or tell you it was not possible, make the choice to shut them out. Even if it was your own family. Create what you desire. Determine to be above your fear. Hold onto your faith. Have a grateful mind. Prefer to hold onto your purpose. Keep developing your talents which are necessary for your desired work.

Choose not to let your fear kill your dreams. Yes, you may fail at times. Perhaps multiple times. Keep going! It only takes one success to bring a change into your life. Imagine all those one-hit wonders or inventions surrounding us.

As was written above, your time was limited. Never stop. Time was precious. You have tremendous power. Show the world your light. Keep thinking big, my fellow readers. If need be, watch videos, read books, or attend conferences. Retrain your mind. Embrace not to settle. It was never too late.

I drifted off into deep slumber.

Campground by A Lake

CHAPTER 47

APRIL 26, 2016

I awoke in the middle of the night once, partly because I was cold, and I had to use the bathroom. After the bathroom break, I curled up again in the back of the truck. I did not wake again until after the sun rose, about 8:30 a.m.; normally not the case during the tour. I had been waking up around 6:30 a.m. along with multiple awakenings during the night.

I was blessed I could access the WiFi from the parking lot. I could catch up on my emails as well as social media. After the updates, I entered the Wal-Mart to brush my teeth and eat some breakfast. As I exited the parking lot, I noticed signs stating overnight parking was not allowed. It was posted on the outermost light poles. I had not seen those the night before. It was the first time I had seen those types of signs at a Wal-Mart since I had departed

Mississippi. I did notice a van parked a few spots from me, which had also been there overnight.

Next, I drove toward the Skagit Valley. The short drive was charming. I was returning to the mountains. Originally, I had planned to stay at a state park in the area. Unfortunately, I accidentally missed the turn. Based on the road atlas, I knew there was a road not too far away offering some free camping by a lake. As I started up the road, I allowed myself 10 miles to find any side roads which may provide safe, free overnight camping. I traveled past a couple of campgrounds along the route.

At the 10-mile mark, I ventured up one gravel side road. After about two miles, I turned around to head back to a campground I had seen by a lake. It offered limited facilities: a port-a-john only, no showers, but it was next to an enchanting lake. Each campsite contained a picnic table, fire ring, and privacy. The cost was $7 per night. Needless to say, I decided to stay. After unpacking and constructing my camp, I wrote for a while sitting at the picnic table looking over the alluring lake. Snow-capped mountains were the backdrop.

I figured how far away I was from Mississippi. It seemed so close. However, on the map I was over 2,600 miles away. I had to drive at least five hours a day to make it back in time for the awards show. It also meant I would not be able to sightsee as much on the way home. Most importantly, I would not have as many opportunities to perform as I had hoped for. The Hard Rock Café performance might have been the last. *Given all the complexities of planning I'd been through just getting myself from place to place, my hat was off to tour managers who set up an entire tour for a major musical act. Their individual members needed rooms, food, and other necessities. With the knowledge to plan the trip so smartly, everything would fit together perfectly.*

In my ideal world, I would continue the journey for the rest of my days. It was my bliss. Traveling, writing, and performing. I continued to pray those seeds I'd been planting allow an abundant harvest of rewards enabling me to always follow bliss.

Awe-inspiring Mother Nature

CHAPTER 48
APRIL 27, 2016

I gazed into the camp fire for over four hours the previous night before turning in. The frogs were croaking in the background as a few stars squeezed through the clouds to shine. The temperature was not too bad as I sat there. I pondered about following my bliss and living my life as if I could not fail. *I enjoyed what I had done. I prayed I could continue to live life daily for the rest of my days, listening to my heart.*

I had tossed and turned some the night before in the truck. I was awakened by a rainstorm. I guess I had not smoked enough blue haze to make me shrink in size like it did the last time.

I awoke to a gentleman setting up his RV in the spot next to me. I was surprised when I realized it was almost 9:00 a.m. I decided not to rush off. I prepared bacon and eggs for breakfast. I remained in the present moment. I enjoyed the nature surrounding me. I slowly packed my things away after taking my sponge bath and dressing in clean clothes.

It was the first day I had to begin driving at least five hours to return to Mississippi in time for the awards show on May 6th. It still did not feel like I was far away from home. Yet when I looked at the map, I had 2,500 miles or more to go. It meant I probably would not have an opportunity to perform again like I was hoping. The time was slipping away from me.

The day's drive was intriguing. The landscape changed so much as I drove. I began the day heading up into the mountains. I saw waterfalls along with the remnants of winter snow. I stopped and snapped a picture by a snow bank almost as tall as I was. The roads were clean and dry. I was told they had just opened the pass about a week before. As I descended on the route, I found myself driving through farmlands, rivers, streams, and then back again up into the mountains. I reveled in the diverse landscapes.

I located a free campsite by a beautiful river where I could spend the night. I was 10 miles off the beaten path in the mountains by the river. I did not arrive until after 7:00 p.m. I had to hurry to set up the campsite before darkness arrived. Normally, I liked to be set up by 5:00 p.m. so I could read and not be rushed due to darkness. I noticed a few campfires along the river in the distance. There was a person camping across from me too. For dinner, I prepared a chicken stir fry as I sat by a campfire. The river created a peaceful atmosphere. The stars illuminated the sky. Sadly, it was too cold to remain outside to gaze upon them. As I lay curled up in my sleeping bag typing, I heard turkeys and coyotes in the background. From my previous experience with the raccoon, I knew not to leave food out near the truck. It could attract wild animals. I also slept with my gun. Parking all alone in those locations, I wanted to ensure it was readily available. I was camping in places which were considered remote. I was all alone. I said my prayers nightly, asking for safety, because I was traveling during the off-season for camping. Though I might be near or inside a public campsite, there was no one around me for the most part. In almost all those locations, the cell phone had no service due to lack of signal. I had faith, always; I was safe, secure, and okay.

As I moved forward on the "Confessions of a Dreamer Tour," I traveled farther than I had before. I required five hours of driving or more compared to earlier of three to four hours. I planned to remain on two-lane roads. The day before, I had chosen US-2-E instead of I-90 East. I wanted to witness the beauty of America which people miss by traveling the Interstate.

I would arrive in Spokane, Washington the next day. It was about an hour from where I was camping. I needed an oil change and my tires rotated and balanced before moving on. I hoped it would remove the vibrating steering wheel. I would also search online for open mics. Busking on the streets might be over due to the limited time remaining as well as the colder weather.

I remained faithful I could live my life like this daily. I enjoyed traveling, writing, performing, and sightseeing. Perhaps ultimately, I can inspire you to follow your bliss and live the life you want, to live like you cannot fail. Or at least get you out on the road to visit some of those sights I had seen.

Last Night
Free Camping Sight
Grand Coulee River, Washington

CHAPTER 49
APRIL 28, 2016

I had a challenging night. I was unable to fall asleep. I was not cold, My mind was just filled with thoughts, desires, and requests; sprinting with images of success as an author, a songwriter, and world traveler blogger. Suddenly I would switch to dangers lurking outside of the truck as I sat alone with no one around me for 10 miles on my side of the river. It seemed I was awake for over three hours before drifting off to slumber. If I had been at home, I could have gotten up to do something like write or practice guitar. However, in the back seat of the truck, all I could do was lie there in dark silence. Every time my eyes opened, I saw darkness. I thought I had one more good nap in me before the sunrise. I checked the clock, it was only 3:45 a.m. - another two-hours before sunrise. I thought about leaving, but I did not want to drive in the dark and miss scenery or, worse, take a wrong turn. I finally slipped back to sleep. When I awoke it was around 7:30 a.m. The morning light outside penetrated the truck's front glass. I wanted to lie there curled up in the sleeping bag for a while, as I was exhausted. Instead, I arose to begin the morning. I noticed my right eye was hurting. It was irritated for an unknown reason. I prepared breakfast, then I ate overlooking the flowing river. It was peaceful and serene. After the meal, I packed my things quickly. I knew I needed to hit the road. The drive out was stunning. It was a wonderful place where I would have enjoyed staying a few days to rest, relax, and cherish the surrounding beauty and serenity.

The day's first destination was Spokane, Washington. The oil light had been illuminated over the past several days. The steering wheel began to vibrate the week before when driving between 30 to 40 mph. My thought was it was due to the rough roads I had chosen. Perhaps the front end was out of balance.

Unfortunately, after the work was completed, the steering wheel remained vibrating. I researched and found the issue may be caused by a poor spark plug. I guessed it was finally time for some new spark plugs. With the daily drive of almost 300 miles a day, playing music was not at the forefront of my thinking. As the oil was changed, I read in the local paper about an open mic taking place later that night. However, when I visited the website, it listed no details about it. So, instead of remaining in Spokane, I decided to resume heading east.

APRIL 28, 2016

Overall, Spokane offered a lot of nightlife. It was home to Gonzaga University. I probably could have located lots of places to perform there on a weekly basis. Though, from what I could see while I was driving around, it was not a place I would like to live.

I was forced to drive on I-90 East for over an hour after leaving Spokane. I continued looking at the map and GPS on the phone to find another two-lane blacktop to keep me heading east. I located a road near Wallace Mullan, Washington I could transition to. It allowed the return to going off-the-beaten track. When Highway 4 ended, there was no highway 471 like the map showed. It was only mountain trails. So, it was back to the 90-East Interstate. I kept my eye on the map, looking for campgrounds, as I only wanted to drive about two to three hours once I left Spokane.

I crossed the state line into Montana. I immediately saw I was driving next to the River St. Regis. It was an incredible sight. Thoughts of kayaking the river consumed my imagination. My first attempt to locate a campground was near the exit for Henderson, Montana. Unfortunately, it was closed. The campgrounds I found were all closed. At first, I did not understand why. The snow was gone. The temperatures for the day were in the 60s. The skies were clear and blue. I later learned the major campgrounds did not begin operation until May. At least searching for those campsites kept me off the Interstate. The roads I used while searching for a campsite were mostly hard-packed gravel. I saw about a dozen deer as well. Finally, I had to abandon the idea of camping. Darkness was promptly arriving. I wanted to be out of the truck before it occurred. I decided to find a hotel room in Missoula, Montana, which was an added one-hour 27-minute drive along the interstate. It was probably a blessing. I was tired. I had not taken a shower in three days. My right eye was red and inflamed. I did have faith it would heal on its own.

I decided on a Motel 6. The room was quite awesome. It reminded me of the room I had stayed in once, in Paris, France. The room had hardwood floors with simple furniture. I took a long hot shower, then relaxed in a cozy king-size bed. I already sensed an improvement and was re-energized.

The next day would be Friday. Most likely I would journey towards Bozeman, Montana. The next couple of days I planned to focus primarily on driving. Open mics were rarely on weekends. Besides, the weather would not permit busking. I had learned in most of the cities I had visited on the "Confessions of a Dreamer Tour", if they permitted busking, I had to obtain a permit before the performance. I was only busking for a few hours or one day. Paying anywhere from $35 to $150 for a busking or street amp permit in each locale was not feasible.

As I relaxed in the room, a passage by John Bunyan crossed my mind. *"Although you have been through all that*

APRIL 28, 2016

you have, do not regret the many hardships you met. Because it was they who brought you to the place you wished to reach. You carry with you the marks and scars of battles. They are the witnesses of what you suffered along with the rewards of what you conquered. Those beloved marks and scars opened the gates of Paradise."

Keep fighting, readers. I have faith in you. You are filled with power. Continue to remain positive and optimistic. You can create a solid plan. You may experience bumps and bruises along the way. At times, you may need to rest or withdraw from your battle. You are not a coward.

I began my quest in May 2014. "Success consists of going from failure to failure" was once said by an unknown person. Keep grinding.

Have you recognized your path? I believe there was a life reserved for you. By choosing your path, journey, or adventure toward goals, desires, and dreams, you may have nowhere to sleep. Keep reminding yourself it was you who chose to walk the path. The chosen path you walk creates no complaints.

The path was difficult. You may have fallen. You may have gotten bruises or even broken a few bones...a reason why not everyone follows their desired path. I would much rather live to only 40 years of age but LIVE a life, than live to 90 safe and sound with regrets. You have a heart, a soul, and instinct. Trust those voices. Hold onto your vision. Continue your path with a positive attitude. No matter how bad it gets, know you are okay. Believe in yourself always. Look at your life like you have already created your desired reality. Do not be afraid to use your imagination like a child. I have faith in your ability to remain on your path.

Yellowstone River
Livingston, Montana

CHAPTER 50

APRIL 29, 2016

The day was an adventure of trial and error; mostly error. I departed the hotel in Missoula, aiming for the Livingston, Montana area. The drive was almost 230 miles. It was a city about 30 minutes on the other side of Bozeman. I chose it because it was Friday, and I had found I could not perform anywhere in Bozeman on a Friday night.

When I arrived in Livingston, I noticed it was popular for tourists. The town offered numerous attractions. One beloved site was the Livingston Depot. It was constructed in 1902. The Depot was a railroad museum. Another major draw for the city was fly fishing.

I turned onto Highway 89 South. The route went toward Yellowstone National Park. I noticed quite a few free camping areas on the map which I desired to locate. The drive through Bozeman as well as to Livingston was marvelous. The past few days had been filled with out of the world landscapes. No matter where I was, either in the mountains or on the lower plains, there was always something creating awe.

The reason I called this day a day of trial and error was because I went in search of two different free campgrounds. Each one was off the main highway up into the forest region. The first campground I searched for, I drove about five miles into the forest only to find a locked gate. I reached the second campground after driving on a dirt road for about 10 miles. It would have been perfect as the campsites were right next to a stream. But as you already guessed, it was closed as well. It seemed like it was still too early in the season for them to be open.

On the return to the main road toward Livingston, I saw a campsite next to the Yellowstone River. The cost was only $12. It offered no sites by the water as well as no privacy. Instead, I decided to return to the city of Livingston to obtain a hotel room. It was probably the best decision. The night's forecast was to be in the low 30s. Once again, I had heat, a shower, and a comfortable, cozy bed. After walking across the street to eat a Subway sandwich for dinner, I was surprised at how tired I was. I had only performed one writing assignment. I was ready to turn off the lights and enter a dream world.

The room's heater was blasting warmth into the room. With eyes closed, I stated my affirmations. *Continue to use your imagination. Accomplish your goals. See your*

APRIL 29, 2016

dreams into reality. Maintain faith on your path. You deserve to obtain your goals. Choose to walk through the gate to your dreams.

I vowed to see the world each day as if it were the first time. To continue to pursue, no matter the obstacles. It might be challenging. I understood I might lose sleep, fingers might bleed from practicing, I might have hunger pains from a missed meal or might have no roof over my head. I might have to say goodbye to family who were negative. It might be hard. Trust your heart. Listen to your instincts. I believe they guided me safely along the journey.

I understood I might at times fall, stumble, or be told no. It was okay. I would not allow those things to discourage me. Through the lessons I have learned, it only took one success to skyrocket me into a life of abundance.

I continued to remain positive and optimistic. I knew I was dying each day. We all begin to die from the day of our birth. We never knew the day we inhale for the last time. Each day we need to accomplish a goal. You must act!

Readers, I wish you peace, joy, and harmony. Smile, you are accomplishing your goals. The outside world may see you washing dishes, pushing a broom, or selling fries. They do not see the brave warrior who was changing their life one precious moment at a time. Let your desires flow into the world. Show the world how valuable you are. Trust yourself.

Yellowstone National Park
Wyoming

CHAPTER 51

APRIL 30, 2016

I awoke at 6:30 a.m. The bed was not comfortable; it was too soft. The mattress had a lean-to-the-left sensation. I was grateful I had heat last night and covers to keep me warm.

I moved along quickly in packing and checked out of the hotel around 9:15 a.m. I was excited as I was heading towards Yellowstone Park. When I had researched the Yellowstone National Park the night before, I had learned most of the park was closed until the end of May. Much of the park was covered in snow and the bears were transitioning from hibernation. I could drive to Old Faithful. Unfortunately, I would have to backtrack inside the park to exit through a different entrance.

The hour drive to Yellowstone was glorious. I noticed three campsites where I could have stopped the previous evening if I had chosen to continue driving. Highway 89 South ran parallel to the Yellowstone River. It was fast-moving and supposedly unbelievable for rainbow trout. I saw a lot of fly fishermen out there. I drove upon some female elk eating grass by the highway. I paused a few times to snap pictures and to stretch my legs by walking. I saw signs warning I was in bear country. I knew to be careful. The bears had been waking up from hibernation over the past month. They were out looking for food.

I stopped at the Yellowstone visitor's site to ask about open campgrounds along with the best routes to exit the park since there were some closed roads. He was very helpful and told me about certain spots I should not miss along my route for sight-seeing.

Yellowstone Park was well worth the $30 pass, which was good for seven days. The drive towards Old Faithful was majestic. I could only drive between 25 to 45 mph depending upon what section of the park I was exploring. I also had to be careful about animals crossing the road. I saw a lot of animals standing in the middle of the road as well. At one point, I sat in a line of cars for almost 30 minutes as a herd of buffalo walked by. No one blew a horn or tried to go around. Instead, there were lots of camera flashes. I watched elk, deer, and buffalo as I went through the park. I missed seeing a bear at a pull-off section by about 10 minutes.

Old Faithful was interesting. The park rangers gave us the geyser's eruption schedule and told us all times were plus or minus about 10 minutes. As I waited for the famous geyser to erupt, two buffalo came walking by. When Old Faithful erupted, the first spout of water shot up about 150 feet. Then over the next three to four minutes, the flow of water slowly died back down. The steam show was the highlight as it moved across the sky.

On the way out of Yellowstone, I located a path where I could ride my mountain bike. Unfortunately, there was a sign cautioning about a bear sighting just the day before on the path. I had also been told by a ranger someone saw a bear in the area earlier today. I stopped to contemplate whether to walk or ride my bike for at least some of it. The total path was one-mile each way. With my slow walking pace, I could not afford to spend the one to two hours I would need to complete it. Besides, the ranger had told me when one was out in the park at that time of year the risk was much higher of a bear attack. There was not much they could do to prevent it except warn people to be careful and stay away from areas where bears had been seen. I used my better judgment. I did not walk or ride my bike. I really wanted to be set up at a camping site by 4:00 p.m. I wanted to catch up on my reading and my writing assignments. As I departed Yellowstone Park, I told myself I would return one day and stay longer.

As I made my way toward Jackson, Wyoming, I had to drive back through sections of Idaho. The map showed quite a few possible free camping areas and campgrounds. Yet I could not find signs for most of them from the road. Additionally, the ones with signs were all closed. I ventured up into the mountains occasionally on some unknown dirt roads. Sadly, I had to turn around because, due to deep snow on the road, I could not pass through. A mental note to myself was to ensure I had a 4-wheel-drive next time.

I checked out a campground near a town named Drummond. The campsites offered no privacy. Instead, I decided to spend the night in a hotel in Jackson, Wyoming. The overnight temperatures were predicted to be in the low 30s. Luckily, a miracle/blessing occurred. Before arriving at the hotel section outside of Jackson about 30 minutes, I came across a campground by a stream. It was an off-branch of the Jackson Lake. When I drove down to it, I found it was a clear, gravel road to a campsite next to the fast-moving stream. There was still snow on the ground. I thanked God for finding such a marvelous location at the great price of "Free."

To celebrate, I grilled pork chops with some vegetables. I was able to read and write before dark. I sat around the campfire until the stars illuminated. I watched what I believed was a satellite move across the sky. I maintained awareness of my surroundings. I was in bear country. The campsite had a bear box to store food in. I made sure I left no food around as I didn't want to attract a bear during the evening hours. There were a couple of people camping about three football fields from me. The reason the camping site was free was they had not turned on the water to the restrooms yet. The official opening was in May.

I thought about a funny story I had heard earlier in the day, when I was at the Visitor Center for Old Faithful. One ranger was telling another ranger about stopping someone who was busking somewhere in the park. The ranger gave the man a warning. He told him if he continued busking, he would be arrested. The ranger made it sound like it was okay to play music in the park if you didn't ask for money or donations.

Tomorrow was a new day. I was a day closer to my dreams as well as one day closer to Mississippi. I still planned to try to perform at least one to two more times before I returned to Mississippi. The next day was Sunday. The next few days were normal open mic days, possible opportunities. I still had a few cities to pass through. I needed to look at the map regularly to ensure I drove far enough each day to make it back to Mississippi by May 6th.

Dinosaur National Monument
Utah

CHAPTER 52

MAY 1, 2016

I drifted asleep quickly last night. Unfortunately, though, I awoke around 2:00 a.m. I probably stayed awake for about two hours. Then suddenly, I slipped off into a dream. I awoke to blue skies around 8:00 a.m. As I stepped out from the back seat, I noticed frost on the bed cover and camping chairs. It was a brisk 33 degrees. Thankfully, I had not gotten cold during the night. I had put on my thermal underwear before I went to sleep.

I could have remained in the location another day. The splendid clear blue skies, the sound of the fast-moving stream, and the snow-covered ground created a special place. However, with the temperature in the low 30s, it would be difficult to enjoy the day outside. I would be cold the entire time and would hate to waste the day sitting in the truck's front seat running the heater.

Instead, I made my way into Jackson, Wyoming. It was about 20 minutes away. I decided to eat breakfast and locate a WiFi connection to catch up on my social circles. The first thing I noticed when I went online was the detailed interview I had done with Carl Hose about the tour was finally live. As I sat in the McDonald's reading the article, I was overcome with gratitude. The link to the interview had been retweeted and shared on social media. I shared it to all my social networks. I had not checked my online presence the past day or so. While I was eating breakfast, I looked to see what feedback I might have gotten on previous posts.

I originally thought I would make it to Denver, Colorado. As I drove, I realized I had greatly miscalculated the distance. I was only in Utah. Don't get me wrong, the drive was sublime. I drove through snowcapped mountains, twisting and winding curves, up to over 9,000 feet and then down. I saw a lot of wildlife as I drove.

My first encounter of the day was a chipmunk. It was the first chipmunk I had seen since I was in elementary school. Seeing it flooded my mind with memories of my brother, Douglas, and I. When we were growing up on High Rock Lake in North Carolina, we would walk around the neighborhood and hunt for squirrels. Each time we did, we would see lots of chipmunks.

I saw deer again throughout my drive. Some were quite close to the road and did not move as I drove by. I saw my first wild Pronghorn ever. Previously, the only

Pronghorns I had seen were caged at a zoo. To finish off the day, rabbits went darting across the road in front of me.

The goal was to camp again. The map showed numerous campgrounds along the route. Sadly, as had happened on most of the recent trip, I found all the campgrounds in Wyoming were closed. When I reached Utah, I noticed the state parks were open offering a reasonable price of $15 a night to camp. The only downside was they didn't have hot water yet.

I sat there by a lake in Utah with a starry night overhead. I wished I knew the constellations. I was sure they were all present in the sky light above. Mountains created a backdrop of natural color tones. It was windy. I knew the temperatures would dip below freezing. I bundled up to challenge the cold from the back seat.

I recorded a music video of me sitting by the fire under the stars performing my song, "My Guide." I uploaded it to my Tommy Ray Music Facebook page.

I didn't go into a lot of details about the true beauty of the landscapes I had been seeing. I could try and use an increased number of adjectives so when you closed your eyes to visualize, you could see what I saw. I would rather inspire you to get out there yourself. To see with your own eyes by using me as an example. I would like to convey it was never too late to follow your bliss. To reinforce: don't allow money to keep you from chasing your dreams. I was finding out there was always a way to make your dreams come true. I was truly grateful for learning the wisdom I had found. I believed the Universe was guiding me and opening doors as God was providing for my needs. Though I realized when you're chasing a dream, it did need a financial reward. I was looking forward to mine.

Last Night Camping by the Lake
Utah

CHAPTER 53

MAY 2, 2016

I awoke to a stunning blue sky. I had to put on my sunglasses as I was loading up the truck. The sun was so bright, it hurt my eyes. The temperature was pleasant. I removed my headband, jacket, and gloves. I wore only a t-shirt before leaving the campsite by the lake.

I again set the goal to make it to Denver, Colorado. It was the third day in a row I thought I would arrive there. I was surprised to realize I was over 500 miles away.

The drive was tranquil and stunning as can only be imagined. As I had been doing, I remained on a local highway instead of moving forward on the Interstate. During the drive, I was sleepy, which was a common occurrence. I found myself zoning out some on the highway. I zoned out one time, and when I looked up there was a herd of deer on the road. I swerved to the left and thanked God for helping me miss the deer, along with the fact no other car came from the opposite direction. I missed the deer in my lane by only inches at the most. I was traveling about 70 mph at the time. Afterwards, when my heart stopped pounding, I recalled my Uncle James telling me to never swerve, to simply hit whatever was in the way. He had seen more traffic deaths and accidents from swerving to avoid a deer than from the impact of the deer.

I contemplated stopping in Steamboat Springs, Colorado to spend the night. I was having a hard time keeping my eyes open. It was an exciting town. Perhaps it would offer somewhere to perform. The rooms there were not too expensive. Instead, I continued driving. I really wanted to be in Denver. Snow covered the ground for most of the drive through the mountains. The roads themselves were dry and clear. The depth of the snow was over a foot in most places. The roads had multiple switch backs. I could only drive about 20 mph. Unfortunately, I was not able to pull off to snap pictures. The height of the snow banks on the ground in the pull-off areas either blocked views or did not allow room for the truck to park.

I looked up into the mountains from the highway. I could see where people had been skiing and snowboarding in the backcountry away from the commercial ski slopes. I imagined the fun as I wondered how they got up to the heights needed to ski downwards.

I had planned to take a 15-mile detour into the Rocky Mountain National Park to view wildlife when I arrived in Granby, Colorado. I had been blessed to see chipmunks, rabbits, deer, pronghorns, elk, and buffalo on the day's adventure. I would also have liked to see a wild bear, from a safe distance of course. The time was 4:00 p.m. already. If I took the detour, I would have to camp out again. I did not want to arrive in Denver after 7:00 p.m.; my thoughts were it was a waste of money to obtain a hotel room that late. It seemed like I would be cheating myself on time versus the money I paid for the room. I paused for a quick bite and pondered if I needed to go to the grocery store for supplies. I decided to move on to Denver.

I had lived in Grand Junction, Colorado for about eighteen months in 2000. The drive flooded my mind with fond memories of the city along with the experiences I had there. I had played on some incredible golf courses built in the Rockies and in Aspen. I had rollerbladed along the Colorado River through the Glenwood Canyons. I had hiked all the trails in the Colorado National Monument. There was great fresh powder skiing at Powderhorn Ski Resort, rarely packed with people, and with economical fees. I also had fond memories of the friendships I had there and of my church, The Vineyard.

I arrived in Denver finally around 6:00 p.m. I chose to get a hotel room. I had discovered Motel 6's was very accommodating for their price. It was wonderful to be able to take a hot shower, wash my hair, and shave. I caught up on my social media, reading and writing. As the in-room clock displayed 11:00 p.m., I still wanted to accomplish many other tasks before falling asleep.

As I lay in the queen size bed, my mind continued in motion. *I believed in myself. I believed anything, and everything was possible. I had a positive perspective. I had a powerful spirit. It helped me to be brave and courageous.*

I had driven 1,320 miles since departing Seattle. My last performance was at the Hard Rock Café - Seattle. I'd been unable to perform more due to time restrictions. I had about 1,100 miles to go to return to Mississippi on time, which meant I would have to drive about 275 miles or almost five hours a day. I continued looking out for places to perform. There were still a few major cities I would go through on the journey.

I studied the map to see if there were still areas where I would like to camp out or if I would need a hotel room each night for the rest of the way back. If I removed myself from the backroads, I knew I could rely on trusty Wal-Mart parking lots. I wished I could start over and spend more time in most of the places I had visited. It would not only give me more opportunities to perform, but also to participate in the recreational activities I had driven by.

I recalled a passage from *Warrior of the Light*. "*However difficult the object. There is always a way of overcoming your obstacles. You may seek alternative paths. You fill your heart with the necessary determination to face the challenges ahead. If you wait for the ideal moment, you will never set off. It requires a*

MAY 2, 2016

touch of madness to take the first step. To keep moving forward, use the touch of madness."

In 2012, within four months, I had resigned my position in Florida and planned the pilgrimage along the Camino de Santiago. Before departing on the "Confessions of the Dreamer Tour," the decision to resign and move forward was similarly completed in only a few months.

Tommy Ray Music
Rambling Across America

CHAPTER 54

MAY 3, 2016

I awoke in Denver. The day was quite uneventful. I drove the entire day through flat landscapes of Colorado and into Kansas. I stopped in Ellis, Kansas to sleep at a Motel 6.

As I drove, I passed ranch after ranch after ranch. I used my imagination to construct figures in the clouds until they faded away into blue skies. The clouds in the distance resembled mountain peaks.

I used the day's drive to reflect upon my inner perspective. *I knew I could achieve anything. There were miracles all around me. I believed in my abilities. I took risks, but only when my heart told me they were for something worthwhile. I persevered. I was inspired by Helen Keller, who said something similar to my mantra: "There are numerous doors I can open to find my happiness and my dreams. The lesson is not to dwell on the closed ones." I faced everything and rose above it, because I had strength and the will for my dreams to come true. I sensed it. I knew it. I had faith by following my bliss, the money would come. It was already there. I had unwavering faith. I was happy. I was grateful for everything I had. I believed. Nothing was impossible.*

It would soon be a new day. Due to the time restrictions, the day would again be filled with driving. I was beginning to believe the Seattle performance was the last, though it was wondrous. I know I had a lot of future performances ahead of me. Kansas City, here I come.

As you walk, be happy without reason and act happy. Continue to advance. Become all you are capable of becoming. Success in your life was becoming what you desired to be. Be prepared. Be grateful. You have a purpose. Greatness exists in you.

A State of Kansas Ranch

CHAPTER 55

MAY 4, 2016

A slow start. I did not go to bed until 2:00 a.m. the previous night. I had been writing and reading. At 4:00 a.m. I received two text messages in different languages, waking me up. Fortunately, I quickly fell back asleep. I almost did not wake up in time for the 11:00 a.m. checkout from the Motel 6.

The day was spent driving again. I was in Kansas all day. I finally made it to Kansas City and checked into another Motel 6. They were a great value at less than $60 a night.

The highlight of the day for me was having a few drinks with a college friend, Chris. We had gone to Guilford College together. He was a couple of years ahead of me. We were both in the athletic training program. After Guilford College, he went to NC State as a graduate assistant for the football team. After I graduated, I applied for his position, though I was rejected into the NC State's master's program. Instead, I attended Florida A&M University. He went on to attend a Physician Assistant Program at South University in Savannah, Georgia. I once again followed in his footsteps and attended the same program in 2007. He took me out to a unique bar with over 150 beers on tap. I tried two. I was such a lightweight with alcohol; I could not try any others. After a couple of hours of catching up, he dropped me off at the motel. I spent the rest of my evening relaxing in the room reading, writing, and catching up on social media.

I looked at the map. I was slightly over 450 miles away from Southaven, Mississippi. I had two more days to get there. Later I would decide how far I would drive the next day. I had to admit, though, I was tired. Driving fatigued me. I was arriving in the towns well after 5:00 p.m. I had stopped researching open mics. Seattle was my last performance. I was now in drive mode back to Mississippi.

I was exhausted. I truly sensed I was done. I was ready for a break. A future goal was to repeat the adventure, but along the East Coast, heading north towards Vermont, but I needed some time to update my life before deciding on an East Coast route.

I didn't even feel like reading. I simply desired the bed, to curl up under the covers. The next day, I might look for a place to camp before checking into a hotel on Friday. The one thing required for the next day was laundry. I had been wearing the same clothes for two straight days. I had run out of everything.

When fatigue overcame me, I attempted to ground myself once again through breathing and visualization. *I understood I had to rely on myself, my inner strength. I must continue with unwavering faith and love.*

I knew I must go beyond my limitations to strive for goals. Thinking positive thoughts brought them into reality. I imagined my inner strength as a beacon of light. It was bright enough to light up the Universe. I had to trust in myself, to continue the path even on the darkest of days. Have faith you will connect to your inner source. Take the leap!

CHAPTER 56

MAY 5, 2016

I hit a wall last night. My mind was exhausted. Negative thoughts seeped in some. I allowed the EGO to lead for a while. My EGO reminded me again I had not performed since Seattle. I had not street performed since Long Beach, California. I had purchased too many hotel rooms along the tour. To combat my EGO, I loaded the CD series from Rhonda Byrne, *Hero*. The words through the speakers of the truck helped my mind to relax and return to focusing on the accomplishments of the tour. The excitement was building for walking a red carpet at an award's show for the first time ever. I was nominated for two awards. I literally gazed into the rearview mirror and smiled. I had come a long way since arriving in Mississippi in November 2012. In addition, I had made progress in leaps and bounds since May 2014 when I decided to return to my true self to follow my bliss, listening to my heart, along with trusting my instincts.

It was the night before arriving in Southaven for the MSMF Awards. After a full day of driving, I didn't read anything else. I had a simple dinner. I returned to the hotel room. I curled under the covers and drifted off into slumber.

I wanted to simply share with you an inspirational quote from *Warrior of the Light*, an inspiring book I had been using to keep myself focused on my journey: *"I am a Warrior of the Light. I go on long-dreamed-of adventures. I talk out loud to the Angels. I have faith they hear me. I know I have the necessary gifts for my path. I have a destiny to fulfill."*

I pondered the fact we are all going to die. We never know when the day was to come. Each day people depart the earth with no clue today was the day. With the knowledge of how precious life was, we cannot wait until tomorrow. If we say, "I will do it tomorrow," that was where our dreams go to perish. Each day one should be excited to pursue one's goals and dreams. We are merely a flash. Let our flash be a bright moment.

Since I knew I could die at any time, I smiled knowing I had no fear of taking risks. So, what if I was booed or kicked off stage? I had tried. So, what if only 100 people purchased my first E-book? What if one million readers buy the second book? Tomorrow might be the day Tommy Ray Music was licensed for a movie.

MAY 5, 2016

Remain positive, my readers. Do not ponder the outcomes. Simply give your best. Push yourself beyond your limitations. Believe anything and everything was possible. Difficulty may occur. Do whatever needed to continue acting. Never give up. I trust you have the power to obtain your destiny.

CHAPTER 57

MAY 6, 2016

I awoke knowing I was only three hours away from Southaven, Mississippi. I was grateful for the blue-sky day with not a single cloud. I was wearing the same shirt and shorts I'd had on for three days in a row. I needed to do some laundry.

The overall drive was lovely. I laughed when I noticed signs for falling rocks along a highway in Arkansas. The rock-based hill was only about eight feet high. Compare those to the heights in New Mexico, Montana, as well as Colorado. There were a few curvy roads as well. I drove through some of the Ozarks region of Arkansas. I saw lots of places to camp and relax near various bodies of water.

I arrived in Southaven. It was considered a suburb of Memphis, Tennessee. It began from the vision of Kemmons Wilson. He was the founder of Holiday Inn. It was the boyhood home of John Grisham.

I knocked out the to-do list to prepare for the awards show on Saturday night. It included purchasing a tie and socks to match the Italian suit I had purchased in Seattle. I located a laundromat to wash my clothes. Afterward, I cleaned the truck's exterior. I washed away over 3,000 miles of dirt. I visited an ATM. Sadly, my balance was zero. After removing my bank card, I sat in the front seat of the truck, thinking.

"I was letting go and allowing the Universe to answer and provide. I believed doors were opening. Incredible things were materializing. I accepted the help of God; He allowed my dream to guide me towards the tasks life had reserved for me. I chose to walk the path; I had no complaints." (Inspired from Warrior of the Light *by Paulo Coelho).*

I was thinking about my future options. I did not want to remain in Mississippi too long. I loved traveling, writing, and performing. I sat quietly and listened for the answer. I let go. I allowed the next steps to unfold.

I used a credit card to purchase dinner. I returned to the hotel and placed the next day's clothes out to ensure I had everything. The evening was spent watching a few back to back movies.

There was a lot of wisdom and knowledge out there to use to assist us to remain on our chosen path, to accomplish our goals. I have shared many sources throughout the book. There are thousands more. I began my path in May 2014 when I first listened

MAY 6, 2016

to Rhonda Byrne's The Hero *and* The Secret. *I progressed from there with readings of Paulo Coelho. I added YouTube videos to the repertoire. I believe I have made progress. I understand there were no limits. Limits are only in your mind.*

Believe in yourself. Simply try, my friends. Keep moving forward. Keep improving yourself. Continue to focus. Have fun with your imagination. I have faith you are changing your life. Continue to listen to your inner voice. Ignore the haters, even if they are your family. Life was short. Practice urgency.

Everything you have read dealing with words of inspiration along with encouragement was not new. Maybe from a different perspective, intertwined through the "Confessions of a Dreamer Tour." Keep fighting. Keep grinding. Stay on the path of your goals.

Thank you in advance for taking your precious time to read my words. I desired to share my words with the world. To inspire you, to bring value to your lives, to be an example showing anyone can succeed...even a country boy from Zama, Mississippi, with a population of 36 people. I wish you peace and strength.

Day of the Mississippi Music Awards Show

CHAPTER 58

MAY 7, 2016

I awoke drowsy in the hotel room in Southaven. The MSMF Awards Show began at 3:00 p.m. I lounged around until almost 1:30 p.m. My mind and body perceived it was still early in the morning due to my fatigue from the overall tour.

When I arrived at the Landers Center, I saw the red-carpet I was supposed to walk. It had no resemblance to those one sees on TV. No limos. No lines of fans. No one was directing anyone or providing any instructions. I approached the woman snapping pictures to ask about the process. She asked who I was. When I mentioned I was nominated for two awards, she said, "I need your picture taken." I waited my turn. I received my pictures on the red carpet before entering the theater.

Once I was inside the theater, I approached the sound engineer. I had received a schedule of the day's events two days earlier via email. My name was listed next to a time for a five-minute slot. At the time of the original email, I thought nothing of it. After 48 hours expired, my inner voice, or what most call gut instincts, began to think. I believed the time slots were performance slots. I asked him about the schedule. He verified I was on the list to perform during the awards show. I learned that about 15-minutes before the show began! I rushed to my truck to gather my guitar. Luckily, due to my instincts, I'd brought my guitar with me from the hotel. He stated he would try to provide a sound check. I went backstage. Unfortunately, due to sound troubles, a few artists had already taken up the sound check time before I had an opportunity to do mine. When I told others about the situation, they were impressed I was still going to perform with such last-minute notice and no sound check.

The show began. It turned out to be a long evening, as it lasted until about 8:00 p.m. The show consisted of videos on a big screen for the audience, live performances, and the awards themselves.

As the time to perform approached, I walked backstage to prepare. Instead of having me stand on the middle of the stage with a microphone like the other solo artists, the music director asked me to sit to the right of the stage by a Steinway piano. He wanted to break up the monotony of having every solo act just standing on the stage. I never sit when I perform: another interesting variable thrown into the mix. When I first sat on the piano bench, there was no microphone or any input for the guitar. A gentleman came out from behind the curtain with a microphone and set me up. I was positioned so everyone could see me. I had no idea the gentleman helping me was David L. Cook, a 7-time Grammy Award Winner!

During the performance, I forgot a few lines of my lyrics. I performed a hand-picking style instead of with a pick. It created feedback off and on from the speakers to my right. I did not have a monitor. I could not hear my voice. In my mind, the performance was a failure. However, I was complimented afterwards by fellow artists, including David L. Cook.

After the live performances were completed, the awards were handed out. I did not win an award. I was grateful for the nominations, at the very least.

The after-party was relaxing. Only a handful of the artists appeared. I enjoyed a few drinks as well as some wonderful food while interacting with the artists present. Unfortunately, I had to leave early because a migraine occurred. I returned to the hotel to decompress. I took some medicine, turned off the lights, and curled under the covers. I fell asleep knowing the next day I would be back at my Aunt and Uncle's house in Pearl, Mississippi, the starting point.

Live Performance @ 2016 MSMF Awards Show

CHAPTER 59

MAY 8, 2016

I checked out of the hotel at noon. Just like the past few days, my mind and body seemed to feel it was early in the morning. The drive to Pearl was three hours.

As I drove to Pearl, I continued the inner conversation with myself. *I had faith the next door would open as I followed my bliss. I desired to be all in. I desired to live life like I couldn't fail. Which meant I continued to travel, write, compose, and perform. I desired to create value and inspiration for others.*

My mind spiraled at times, meaning I switched thoughts often. One second, I was thinking the above thoughts. And then, without an external prompt, I switched to thoughts of needing to increase the marketing for my first E-book, *A Country Boy on The Camino*. There was a local promotion company in Pearl I could contact about promoting the book.

The next biggest issues to confront me were money and finding a place to stay. As I thought about the next steps, I maintained unwavering faith those were taken care of.

CHAPTER 60

HOME SWEET HOME

The last dated day of the journal. I awoke at my Aunt and Uncle's house in Pearl, Mississippi. To celebrate my safe return, Aunt Jo had prepared a full country breakfast. The aroma of bacon and sausage penetrated the hallways. Scrambled eggs inside the iron skillet with hot fresh biscuits from the oven. The three of us enjoyed conversation and celebrated the triumphant adventure.

As the day unfolded, I thought about the near future. I knew my Aunt and Uncle would allow me to remain with them for as long as I desired. My older brother Douglas would offer the same in Palm Harbor, Florida.

I was patient. I was allowing the Universe to open doors. I had about $1,000 dollars in cash. I had stored the money before I departed on tour. I needed to pay a few bills. I was blessed. I had lots of dreams with the support of most of my *family. We would see how the next few days went and where the adventure led me next.*

I hope you have enjoyed the adventure.
I hope it sparked something inside of you to
find your own adventure.

REFLECTIONS

"Although I have been through all I have, I do not regret the many hardships I met, because it was they who brought me to the place I wished to reach. I carry with me the marks and scars of battles, they are the witnesses of what I suffered and the rewards of what I conquered. These are the beloved marks and scars opening the gates of Paradise to me."

—John Bunyan

The "Confessions of a Dreamer Tour" had completed. As I stated above, I had numerous winding curves. Most goals were completed. Unfortunately, a few were not. Still, I created a plan of action. Then as the plan was carried out, many possibilities arose, forcing me into new directions.

One aspect of the tour I desired to share was the financial aspect. Overall, the cost of the tour was $5,646.82. The cost of food was $754.00. The fuel bill was $1,006.62. Lodging was the most expensive expenditure at $1,522.09. The lodging bill, according to the original plan, was supposed to be the cheapest. Preparation for the tour itself was $1,087.35. Finally, miscellaneous charges were $1,276.76. Those were the suit, cash withdrawals from ATMs, along with truck parts.

"Our deepest fear is not we are inadequate. Our deepest fear is we are powerful beyond measure. It is our light, not our darkness that most frightens us. We ask ourselves, 'Who am I to be brilliant, gorgeous, talented, fabulous?' Who are you not to be? You are a child of God. You're playing small does not serve the world. There is nothing enlightened about shrinking so other people won't feel insecure around you. We are all meant to shine, as children do. We were born to make manifest the glory of God within us. It's not just in some of us; it's in everyone. And as we let our own light shine, we unconsciously give others permission to do the same. As we are liberated from our own fear, our presence automatically liberates others." — *Marianne Williamson, A Return to Love: Reflections on the Principles of "A Course in Miracles"*

For Further Information

www.tommyraybooks.com
Facebook: Tommy Ray Books
Twitter: Tommy Ray Books

www.tommyraymusic.com
Facebook: Tommy Ray Music
Twitter: Tommy Ray Music

www.tommyrayinsights.com
Facebook: Tommy Ray Insights

ABOUT THE AUTHOR

Tommy Ray was born in 1973, in Zama Mississippi, population 36 people. He followed the red dusty dirt road to receive three degrees, each one taking him closer to ever-changing dreams.

However, no matter what he achieved, he always had a voice inside of him telling him he desired to live his life through a creative voice. For many years he ignored the voice to follow other endeavors, but the voice was always there and increasing in volume.

The voice was what made Tommy resign a stable job to go on pilgrimage on the Camino de Santiago in 2012. A pilgrimage in the footsteps of St. James through France and Spain. Though when he returned, he shut the voice out again and returned to the safe norm like so many of us do. In 2016, the voice finally became so loud, he could not take it, so he took another leap of faith. He resigned another position in January of 2016. He journeyed on a self-guided music tour, the "Confessions of a Dreamer Tour."

He chooses to write and became an author to create value and inspiration to the world. He desires all to leave their mark, thinks big, as well as never give up on your dreams. He has always been inspired by travel adventure tales of real-life journeys. He decided it was how he desired to spend his life.

His books are written in a journal style, providing insights as well as glimpses of his fear, pain, joy, and the love which his travels have brought. He plans a series of "A Country Boy" travel adventure books. The goal is to assist readers in dreaming big, listening to their hearts along with trusting their instincts. To take a leap of faith.

DO NOT MISS FUTURE ADVENTURES WITH TOMMY RAY

I ask and invite you to leave a review on the purchasing website as well as Goodreads.

RESOURCES

https://www.youtube.com/watch?v=jJGManTL-1w

https://www.amazon.com/Country-Boy-Camino-Tommy-Ray-ebook/dp/B01HDOTCM2/ref=sr_1_1?ie=UTF8&qid=1499554842&sr=8-1&keywords=country+boy+on+camino

https://www.ascap.com/help/career-development/booking-your-own-tour-a-how-to-guide

http://blog.sonicbids.com/how-to-book-a-diy-tour-like-a-pro

http://diymusician.cdbaby.com/the-diy-musicians-complete-guide-to-touring/

https://www.indieonthemove.com/

https://tinybuddha.com/

www.visitnatchez.com

www.roadtrippers.com

www.thesouthernc.com

www.Facebook.com/eatatnikkis

https://freecampsites.net/
www.reverbnation.com
www.midtownautoservice.net

www.mcgonigels.com

www.franklinbbq.com

www.parks.traviscountytx.gov/find-a-park/hamilton-pool

www.visitwimberley.com/jacobswell

www.sundancesquare.com

www.forthworth.com/listings/fort-worth-cultural-district

www.openmikes.org

RESOURCES

www.thebluelightlive.com

www.albuquerqueoldtown.com

www.nobhillmainstreet.org

https://www.youtube.com/watch?v=YODEINvzrw4&index=8&list=PLz_YO8bEFbvGEAFZeH5PCkzj4i3CdyZJN

www.icecaves.com
https://www.youtube.com/user/rayatc73

www.visitjulian.com

www.reverbnation.com
www.roscoeschickenandwaffles.com

http://madebymillworks.com/

https://www.parks.ca.gov/?page_id=549

http://www.parks.ca.gov/?page_id=536

https://www.nps.gov/goga/planyourvisit/focr.htm

http://www.drivethrutree.com/

http://avenueofthegiants.net/

http://oregonstateparks.org/index.cfm?do=parkPage.dsp_parkPage&parkId=58

http://oregonstateparks.org/index.cfm?do=parkPage.dsp_parkPage&parkId=51

https://www.fs.usda.gov/siuslaw

http://localadventurer.com/thors-well-cape-perpetua-oregon-coast/

http://oregonstateparks.org/index.cfm?do=parkPage.dsp_parkPage&parkId=75

https://www.choicehotels.com/oregon/portland/quality-inn-hotels/or014?source=gyxt

http://thefirkintavern.com/
http://thegoodfoot.com/

http://oregonstateparks.org/index.cfm?do=parkPage.dsp_parkPage&parkId=129

http://www.coastalinnhotel.com

http://www.pioneersquare.com/

http://siggiethevintageman.com/

RESOURCES

www.tommyraymusic.com

http://pikeplacemarket.org/

http://www.kuhlmanseattle.com/

https://www.yelp.com/biz/ian-seattle-5

http://www.emeraldcityguitars.com/
http://www.soulcatguitar.com/

http://www.conorbyrnepub.com/
https://carlhose.wordpress.com/2016/04/30/almost-famous/

https://www.facebook.com/TommyRayMusic

"So...
Be your name Buxbaum or Bixby or Bray
Or Mordecai Ali Van Allen O'Shea,
you're off to Great Places!
Today is your day!
Your mountain is waiting.
So... get on your way!"
— Dr. Seuss